IMAGES
of America

BABYLON
BY THE SEA

LONG ISLAND SOUND

Huntington Bay

Huntington Harbor

NORTHPORT

Main St.

HUNTINGTON

LIRR

H U N T I N G T O N

COMMACK

York Ave.

SOUTH HUNTINGTON

New

Northern State

DIX HILLS

Deer

Long Island Expwy.

HALF HOLLOW HILLS

Park

B A B Y L O N

(Main Line)

LIRR.

DEER PARK

Ave.

WYANDANCH

Southern State

NAT CONKLIN HOUSE

BABYLON

ORIGINAL SITE

LINDENHURST

LIRR (Montauk Div.)

AMITYVILLE

Carll River

Conklin Pt.

(Main St.)

GREAT SOUTH BAY

NASSAU   SUFFOLK

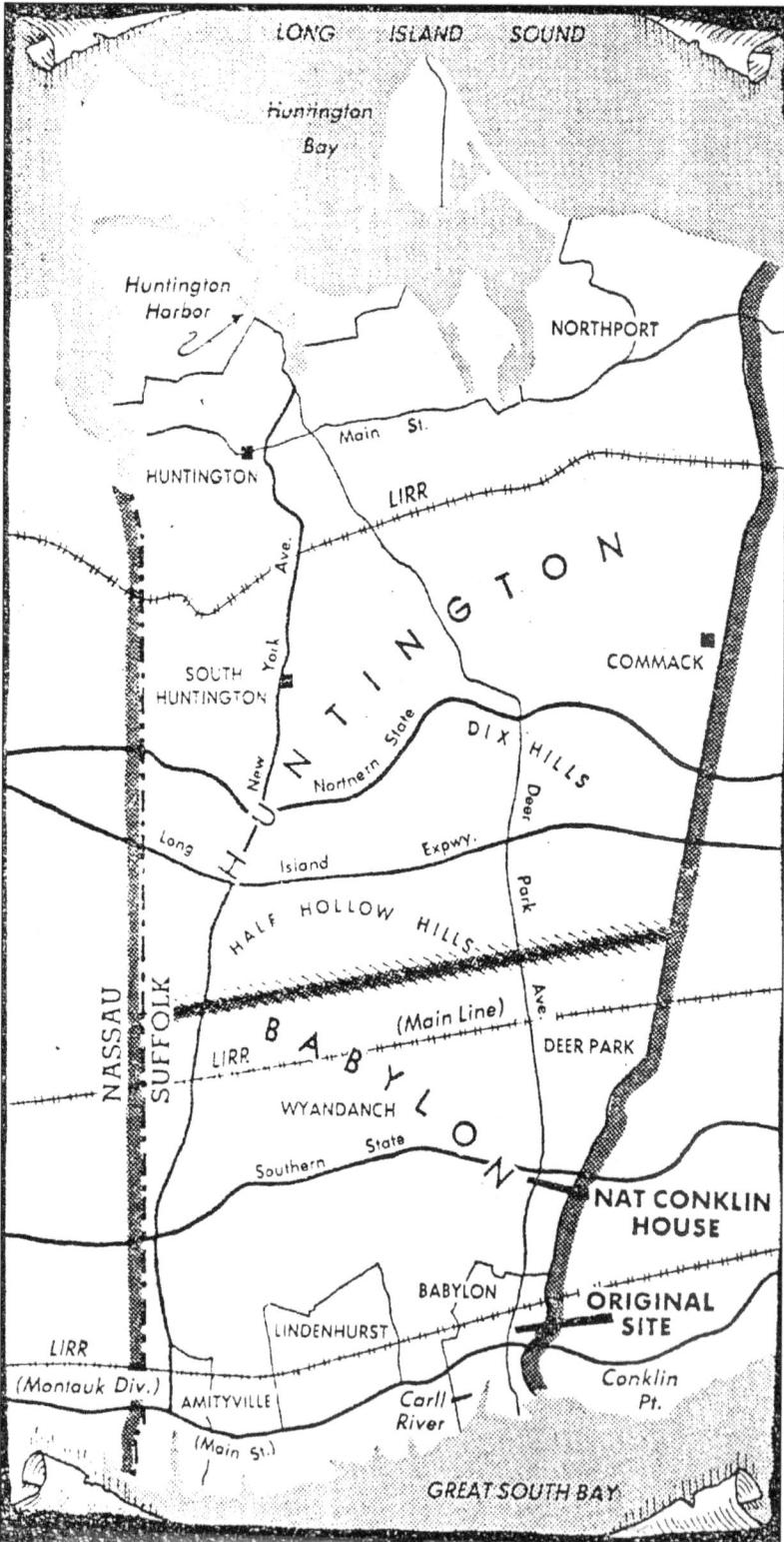

Babylon was originally the southern part of Huntington. Settled in 1689, it was named in 1803 and remained South Huntington until 1872 when citizens voted to separate and form a south shore town. The area along the waterfront became the town of Babylon. August Belmont, financier, horseman, and resident, was one of many forces who strongly advocated independence.

IMAGES
of America

BABYLON
BY THE SEA

Sr. Anne Frances Pulling

ARCADIA
PUBLISHING

Published by Arcadia Publishing
Charleston, South Carolina

Library of Congress Catalog Card Number: 99-62236

For all general information contact Arcadia Publishing at:
Telephone 843-853-2070
Fax 843-853-0044
E-mail sales@arcadiapublishing.com
For customer service and orders:
Toll-Free 1-888-313-2665

Visit us on the Internet at www.arcadiapublishing.com

*Dedicated to the Sisters of Mercy who have ministered in
St. Joseph's School, Babylon, N.Y., during the sixty-four years
of its existence, and to the lay faculty and all the former students
from 1927 through 1991.*

Shaded under their parasol, ladies make their way east on Main Street. This is a turn-of-the-century scene at the intersection of Main Street and Deer Park Avenue. The drinking fountain provided refreshment for man and horse alike. Heffley Drug Store, once the site of the Conklin House, is on the northeast corner. The spire of the Presbyterian Church, in the background, has long been a landmark in the village of Babylon.

CONTENTS

Sunset forms a magnificent spectacle on the rippling waters of the Great South Bay. It creates a panoramic view of Fire Island Bridge from the hilly, sandy marshes. Fire Island Bridge connects Captree State Park with Robert Moses State Park on Fire Island. The bridges link the mainland with the glimmering beaches on the Atlantic Ocean. The area is frequented in summer for recreation and often in winter for its majestic and charming winter seascapes.

Acknowledgments

This publication is based on research, records, periodicals, documents, newspapers, and interviews with townsfolk knowledgeable about local history, many of whom graciously supplied information and offered constructive suggestions. A special thank you goes to The Village of Babylon Historical and Preservation Society, especially Alice Zaruka and Ruth Albin for sharing many photographs and a wealth of knowledge.

A word of gratitude goes to Leo Murphy and Patricia Vandette of the Ancient Order of Hibernians, Fred Van Bourgondein, Ron Ziel, the Dominican Sisters of Amityville, and Seth Purdy of the Amityville Historical Society. A thank you goes to Michael Lobasso, principal of Babylon High School; New York State Office of Parks, Recreation and Historic Preservation; Gayle Haines, who shared knowledge of the bay; John Anthony's on the Water, and Hapi Auer of Glen's Dinette, who shared his photographs of old-time Babylon.

Prayerful gratitude goes to all who assisted in any way by supplying photographs, constructive suggestions, assistance with captions, proofreading, etc. I am especially grateful to my own religious community, The Sisters of Mercy of the Dallas Regional Community for their support and encouragement in this project.

INTRODUCTION

Babylon is a seaside community on the south shore of Long Island. Originally called Sumpwams, it was once part of Huntington. The story of Babylon began to unfold when north shore pioneers discovered the salt marshes along Great South Bay. Salt hay was needed as bedding and food for the livestock. Frontiersmen built crude shelters near the bay while harvesting hay, hunting, fishing, and clam digging. The first purchase of land took place in 1670.

Gradually a little settlement evolved along South Country Road. Among our earliest settlers was the Conklin family, who came from Huntington. Phoebe Conklin gave the area its name. The location of her son's home prompted a response that would forever identify this vibrant, prosperous, thriving town and village on Long Island's Great South Bay. The settlement gained distinction as a summer resort when Fire Island became popular with the elite of New York City. Many wealthy and fashionable folks came in quest of the invigorating air and relaxation away from the city. Hotels and boardinghouses sprang up around the village. Fire Island, the last outpost on this continent, separates Great South Bay from the Atlantic Ocean. A lighthouse was built on the western tip of Fire Island in 1827 to curtail shipwrecks. In 1855 David Sammis built his famous Surf Hotel on Fire Island Avenue to transport city dwellers to the waterfront. They then boarded a ferry for a cruse across the bay to the Surf Hotel.

The Revolutionary War touched Babylon in 1778. The original Presbyterian Church, built in 1730, was demolished by British occupation forces and the materials taken to Hempstead where they were used in constructing barracks for British forces stationed there.

A picturesque windmill once stood at the railroad depot. It filled the tanks for watering engines and became an early landmark. The Argyle Hotel produced one of the nation's first all black baseball teams. Headed by Frank Thompson, headwaiter, it was formed in 1885 by the waiters and busboys at the hotel.

In 1892 the government designated Fire Island a receiving station for European ships carrying diseased immigrants. This caused a rebellion as townsmen threatened to destroy the ships. Finally a militia was sent to guard the waterfront. Gugliemo Marconi, the Italian inventor, contacted ships at sea by wireless from Babylon. Electricity for general use was initiated in Babylon, and it was the first village to have streetlights. In 1925 the South Shore line of the railroad was electrified to Babylon. This meant speedier, efficient service between the metropolis and the village. It also brought a myriad of daily commuters from surrounding areas. Robert Moses, genius of the park system, made his home here, as did Robert Keeshan, whose fame as Captain Kangaroo lies in his theory of education through amusement.

The town of Babylon consists of three villages, and eight hamlets each with its own distinctive character. The total population of 205,000 inhabitants is divided among the Incorporated Villages of Babylon, Amityville, Lindenhurst, and the unincorporated settlements. Among these, Copiague, nestled between Lindenhurst and Amityville, derives its name from the Native American word meaning "sheltered place." Situated on the bay, it was home to a touch of Venice. In the 1920s a bandstand, bridges, and pillars, modeled after the Italian City, were constructed along the grand canal.

The quaint little village of Babylon measures only 1 mile east to west and 2 miles north to south. Classic white church steeples pierce the landscape and provide a backdrop for the old-time Main Street accent. Victorian lampposts line the Main thoroughfares with suspended seasonal displays. The familiarity factor is strong in the village of Babylon.

Deer Park is an inland settlement in the scrub oak and pine belt area. In 1842 the main line of the railroad reached Deer Park, and it became a point of convergence where stage and rail met. Passengers were transported to and from the American Hotel in Babylon. This was a stage stop for many years. In 1835 President John Quincy Adams made Deer Park his summer home. In 1916 the Long Island Agricultural and Technological Institute was established in Farmingdale on the Nassau-Suffolk border, and in 1948 it became part of the State University of New York.

Long Island is the cradle of aviation. In the 1940s East Farmingdale gained prominence when Republic Aircraft Factory turned out fighter planes for the Second World War. The plant provided employment for numerous defense workers. The world's first seaplane was designed in Farmingdale by Lawrence Sperry, an aviation pioneer who tested it in Amityville.

Babylon of Biblical fame is situated on the Euphrates River near present-day Iraq. It was ruled by King Nebuchanezzar, who made it one of the seven wonders of the Ancient world. In his quest for power he invaded Jerusalem, burned the temple, captured the Jews, and exiled them into far off Babylon. They were held captive for many years, hence the name Babylon took on an adverse connotation.

In Babylon on Great South Bay that image has been reversed. Ours is a thriving, pleasant town where peace and harmony reign. Hopefully, in the new millennium this pictorial rendition will recapture and preserve Babylon's colorful, harmonious past for future generations and afford a glimpse of yesteryear into *Babylon by the Sea*.

—Sr. Anne Frances Pulling

One

SALT MARSHES
OF LONG AGO

The salt meadows along the bay drew settlers from the north. The area became South Huntington as early pioneers tramped out a path, now Deer Park Avenue, to the salt marshes to harvest salt hay. The hay was used as feed and bedding for the livestock. Originally, frontiersmen built crude shelters for themselves while harvesting hay, hunting, fishing, or clam digging. The first purchase of land in what is now Babylon took place in 1657.

Phoebe Conklin, an avid Bible student, gave Babylon its name. Her son, Nathaniel, built this house beside the American Hotel. In exasperation she exclaimed, "It will be another Babylon," and he replied, "It will be a New Babylon." Its proximity to the sea combined with her recollection of biblical Babylon in Psalm 137, prompted this reply. His response was etched on a tablet placed in the chimney of his home.

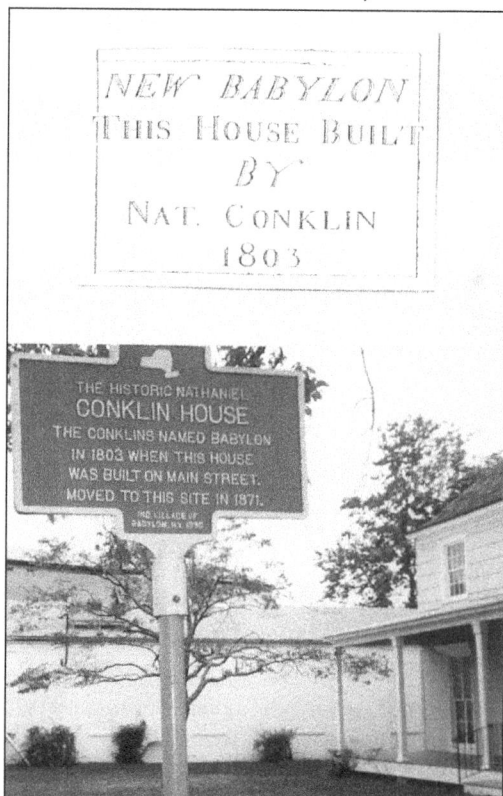

The stone tablet, originally in the chimney of the Conklin House, was found when the house was relocated. Still bearing the inscription, it is preserved in the library. The village took over the Conklin building and placed an historical marker in front of the house when it was designated an historical landmark. This is the only town in the United States bearing the name Babylon.

The Conklin House was moved north to Deer Park Avenue in 1871. It stood beside the Washington Hotel in its new location. In 1910 it became a popular boardinghouse for workers on Sunrise Highway. In 1945 the Sammis family deeded it to the Red Cross. It is currently under restoration as a center of historical, cultural, and educational activity.

Nathaniel Conklin established a tannery on east Main Street in 1800, approximately where Bayview Rest Home is now. It operated until 1861.

The Old Mill was built in 1750 at the eastern entrance to Babylon Village for Judge Gerrett Montford. It was later owned by Nathaniel Conklin. When David Rickett, second president of Babylon, took it over, it became a toy whip factory. The mill was situated on Sumpwams Brook, north of Main Street. The Oakley family operated it as a gristmill for over a half century. Edward Hawley had it razed in 1910.

Southards Gristmill was located at the west end of present-day Southard's Lane in Babylon. Southard operated the mill for many years. He cleared a grove on his property and built a platform for picnics, parties, and dancing. It was called Lake Grove Park, and it catered to summer festivals. It is now part of the Long Island State Park Trail.

Dr. John Scudder and family were among Babylon's earliest settlers. The snows fell abundantly over Long Island in earlier times. It always provided opportunity to enjoy the beauty of a winter landscape and the necessity of a sleigh.

A two-wheeled gig traveled along Main Street. This light, one-horse carriage belonged to Dr. John Scudder, who found it feasible to hitch up the gig and make his calls. Many of his calls were to outlying districts where wheels were a necessity.

The First Presbyterian Church was established in 1730. The present site was chosen in 1784. In 1838 the church was moved to an adjoining lot and became a dwelling. The population continued to increase, and in 1870 the present church was constructed. It conveys an aura of simplicity and warmth. The 250-foot spire, with its clock tower and minaret steeple, has long been a landmark and beacon to those on land and on sea.

The home of David S.S. Sammis, proprietor of the Surf Hotel on Fire Island, was once the Second Presbyterian Church. Built in 1790, it served as a house of worship for a half century. In 1838 it was moved a few feet east and became the home of the Sammis family. In 1951 the building again became part of the parish, and today it houses offices. It is one of the oldest buildings in the town of Babylon.

14

The blacksmith shop stood on the west side of Deer Park Avenue, behind the American Hotel. Andrew Titus was its first proprietor, and in 1870 Treadwell Smith became the village blacksmith. The forge was a vital necessity in pioneering times and served the village hotels as well as its citizens.

South Country Road connects Queens County and Montauk Point. Tramped out by Native Americans, it followed the ocean for over 100 miles. South Country Road has become Main Street for many villages along the waterfront. It is also known as Montauk Highway. The carriage of 1800 is traveling west into Babylon along the tree-lined road. The bay is a mile to the left.

The George Keyser family enjoys a leisurely drive along Main Street. They came to Babylon in 1898 and established a florist on Little East Neck Road, which is still in operation. The florist has changed hands over the years but the name remains.

A turn-of-the-century clambake in Keysers Woods was equivalent to a picnic today. A chicken wire fence contained the property located in the woods behind Keysers greenhouse establishment. Clambakes were common in the early days, especially along the waterfront.

16

James B. Cooper Sr. was county clerk, a justice of the peace, and a well-known historian. His father, Simeon Wheeler Cooper, brought the family to Babylon in 1804, established a tannery on Main Street, and became second postmaster. The family home was settled across from the Presbyterian Church. The property, northeast of Montauk Highway, was laid out into streets named for his sons: James, George, and Simeon. Cooper Street, named after James Cooper Sr., ran parallel to Deer Park Avenue.

James B. Cooper II was employed by the South Side Signal. In July 1911 he founded the *Babylon Leader* and in 1927 the *Lindenhurst Star*. He completed his father's term as justice of the peace when the latter died in 1911. As village clerk he led a successful movement to open Shore Drive, paralleling Sumpawms River, and to extend other highways to the bay.

The Carll homestead was located west of the American Hotel on the north side of Main Street. Built in 1826 by Selah Smith and Julia Carll, it had five open fireplaces. Citizens to whom she was most generous dubbed the house "Aunt Julia's house." Julia was the daughter of Judge Issac Thompson of West Islip and the mother of Timothy, who later operated a successful fabric business.

This is the Hulse house, built on the southwest corner of James Street and Totten Place. Daniel Totten, for whom the street was named, was a haberdasher who arrived in 1824. His home and business were on Main Street. He established a prosperous business designing and manufacturing hats made of beaver fur. He earned a fortune on his beaver hats. The industry phased out when a change in style became the fad.

18

The Methodist Church has stood on the northeast corner of Deer Park Avenue and James Street since 1859. A tiny structure had been erected near Grove Place; however, the congregation rapidly outgrew it. William R. Foster donated land for a new church. Completed in early American Gothic architecture, it conveys an atmosphere of composure and peace. The parsonage stands beside the church.

The First Baptist Church of Babylon stood on the northeast corner of Main Street and Carll Avenue. Built in 1873 it served the Baptist congregation for over eight decades. In 1958 a new church edifice was constructed farther west on Main Street, and the site of the church has become a parking lot, which serves the municipal building, police department, and historical society. Note the spire of the Presbyterian Church as one looks east on Main Street.

19

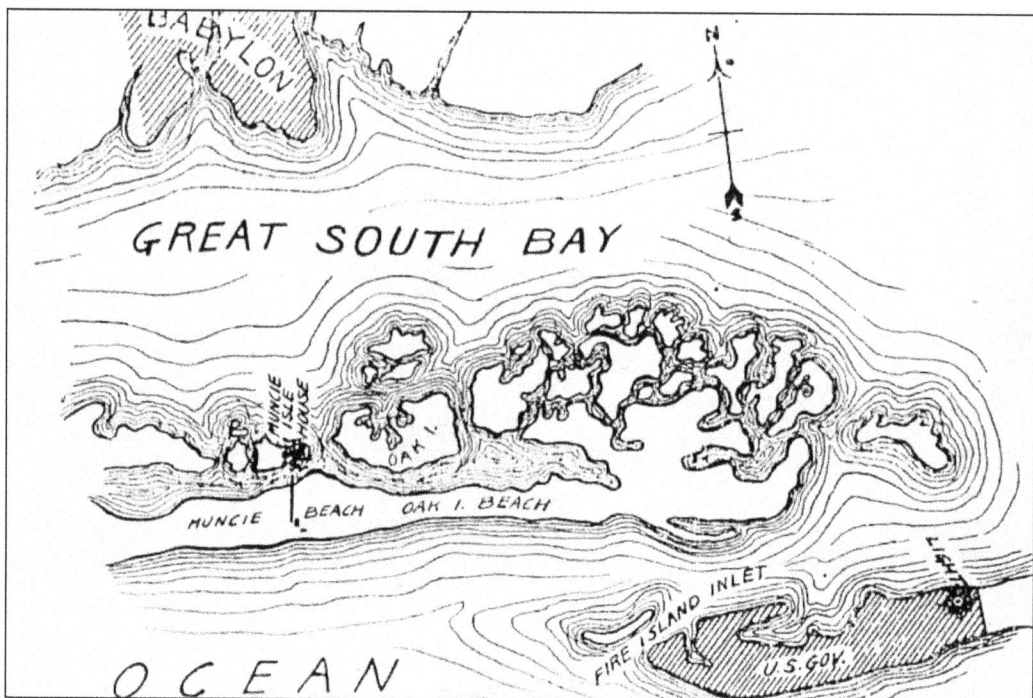

The ocean broke through the barrier beach at Fire Island Inlet. The date is uncertain; however, the action took a wide sweep of marshlands and created Great South Bay. Note the distance of the lighthouse from the western tip of Fire Island at Democratic Point. Dredging is now necessary to keep the inlet open. The pounding of the surf, storms, and tidal activity have changed the shoreline and extended Fire Island westward.

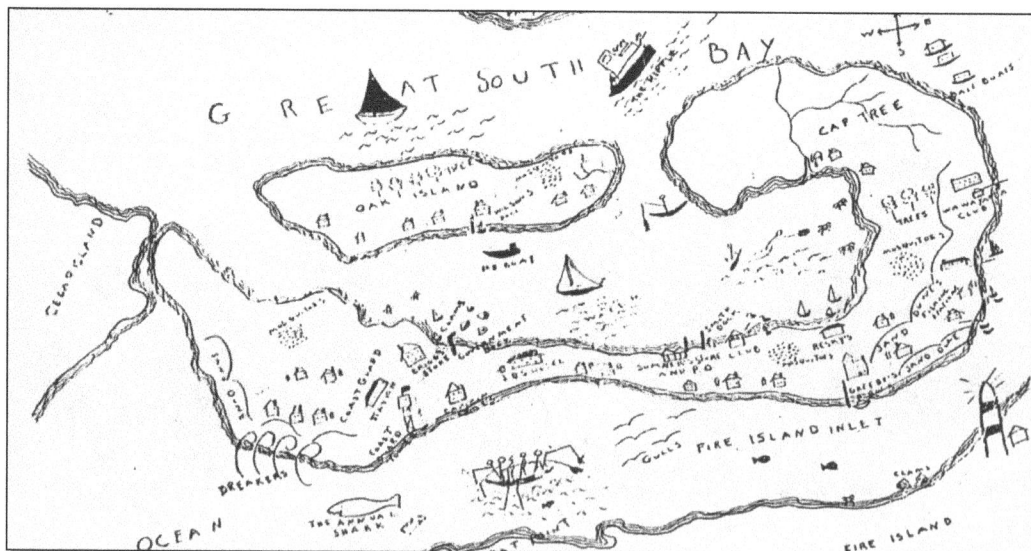

The restless sea is in constant, erratic motion. The result is a continuous change on the frontage of the barrier beach. Note the distance of the lighthouse from the western tip of Fire Island in this 1931 photo. Breakers, those waves breaking into foam on the shore, constantly transform the shoreline. Long Island's South Shore is protected from the pounding of ocean waves. This is where, why, and how the Babylon story began.

Two

FRINGED IN SAND

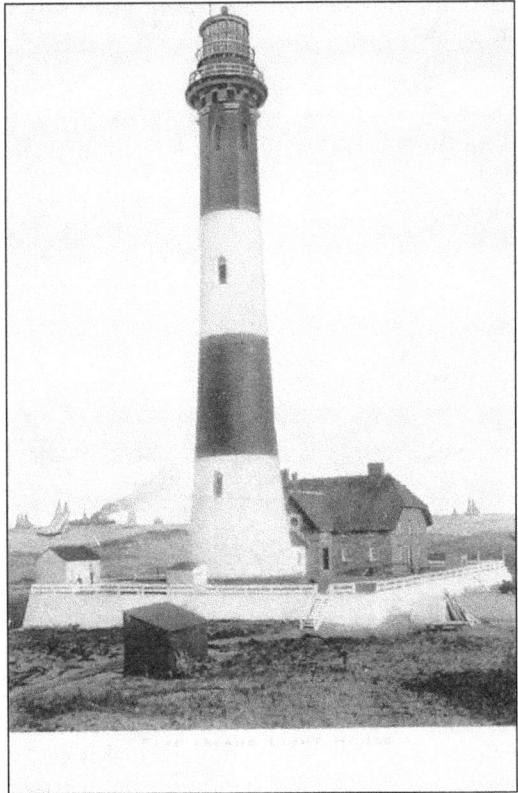

The Fire Island lighthouse has been guiding ships as they approach and depart New York Harbor since 1827. Frequent shipwrecks prompted the federal government to erect a lighthouse on the western tip of Fire Island just east of the inlet. In 1858 the present and higher lighthouse was erected near the same site. Restored in 1986 it rises 167 feet with a coastal navigational beacon flashing every 7.5 seconds around the bay and out to sea.

Fire Island is a 32-mile strip of barrier beach parallel to the southern coast of Long Island. In 1964 it became a National Seashore, which assures it protection from commercialism. This coastal lighthouse is often the first sight of America for ships coming from Europe. Fire Island separates the bay from the ocean. High winds drift the sand into high dunes and spectacular shoreline designs.

A keeper was originally required to keep the lighthouse lamp aglow. Felix Dominy, the second keeper, created a pattern of informal boarding in 1836. Small groups of visitors came, enjoyed his adjacent summerhouse, dined, and stayed overnight. A new concept slowly evolved. When he retired in 1844, he opened the first hostelry for paying guests and thus launched the idea of seaside hotels. The first lighthouse keeper was William Temple.

The Fire Island Ferry cruised Great South Bay for many years. It was a light vessel and among the first ferries on the bay. It transported passengers to the beaches on Fire Island. This strip of white quartz sand has been attracting people for centuries. The first ferry to make regular trips across the bay began with D.D. Sammis in 1856.

Fire Island Avenue is a connecting link with the Great South Bay. It was part of the Underhill Farm and was originally called Placide Street in memory of a popular New York comedian. When Babylon Dock was established at the foot of this thoroughfare, most passengers were bound for Fire Island. It seemed fitting to assume the name Fire Island Avenue. This was before the trolley tracks were laid.

Electus B. Litchfield established his estate on Argyle Lake in 1864. He was a railroad financier from Brooklyn, who called the area Blythbourne. In 1810 it was the site of Timothy Carll's fabric manufacturing business. In 1849 Issac Willetts manufactured straw paper on Argyle. Captain Brewer, a retired sea captain, purchased the property before Litchfield bought it and set up his estate here. Austin Corbin lived here while his palatial mansion was under construction.

Austin Corbin, president of the railroad, built the Argyle Hotel in 1882. He bought the 15-acre lake site and had this 300-room mansion constructed in Queen Anne style. He had solicited English investors for his project, and the Duke of Argyle was among them—hence the name. Corbin entertained President Chester A. Arthur in this luxurious setting.

A trolley crosses Argyle Lake for the convenience and pleasure of patrons. Bound for Babylon Dock it provided transportation to the ferry and the ocean. Freshwater swimming was available at Argyle, but some preferred ocean bathing. This required a short trolley ride to the sea. Argyle Lake is formed from one of the many freshwater streams in the area.

Cottages dot the landscape at Argyle. There were 14 cottages surrounding the mansion. In 1896 the mansion that held such promise experienced financial failure. Corbin sold his interests to William Zigler, the Royal Baking Powder king. In 1904 the mansion was razed and the lumber went into the construction of 20 modern cottages on scattered sites around the grounds. Many of these cottages have become permanent residences.

The barrenness of late winter has a beauty all its own. The leafless trees sway in late winter winds, and the lake is in peaceful readiness for the coming spring. Note the gazebo and cottages in the background. A small white bridge enhances the north side of the lake. This was a postcard sent to the Linwood Inn in Bay Shore from Babylon early in the century.

Swans flock to the water's edge when they suspect a treat. Argyle Lake continues to be a peaceful place that the wheels of progress have not touched. A few feet away life rushes on; however, on the lake a peaceful atmosphere prevails. Swans and ducks glide across the waters, sometimes calling to each other. One can easily become wrapped in solitude on the calming waters of Argyle Lake.

26

The gazebo was part of Argyle's panorama in its heyday. Flowering walks, pleasant drives, and tree-lined lanes all added to the pleasure, entertainment, and relaxation of those patronizing the Argyle. A small measure of that atmosphere has been maintained around the little roadways that weave through the area today.

The Argyle Lake overflow is situated on the north side of Montauk Highway. In its artistic setting, the waterfall provides an ideal backdrop for wedding and anniversary pictures. Many such parties avail themselves of this picturesque setting.

5423   ENTRANCE TO HAWLEY'S PARK, BABYLON, L. I,   ILUST. POST CARD CO., N. Y.

Artistic gates enclose Hawley Park and estate at the eastern entrance to Babylon village. Edwin Hawley, a railroad executive and magnate, bought the Effingham Sutton estate and developed it.

Effingham Park was the estate of Sutton Effingham, who was a New York merchant in the dry goods business. He came in 1870 after having made a fortune by introducing a fleet of clipper ships. His home was on the east side of the pond that once graced the southern terminus of present Route 231. His private park included the pond and three cottages. He was a staunch benefactor of Christ Church.

28

Hawley's Pond formed part of the Effingham estate east of the village. The overflow of the pond was constructed to match the Argyle overflow west of the village. The falls were situated on Montauk Highway approximately between the east-west forks of Route 231. Edward Hawley was a railroad tycoon.

J.J. Robbins provides a glimpse of two grand hotels. The Argyle is shown above, with lake, landscaping, and train chugging past the front door. The Surf Hotel on Fire Island, below, is surrounded by rowboats, sailboats, steamers, and ferries. Both hotels catered to the prosperous of New York. The Argyle featured a grand ballroom, casino, and a nightly orchestra from June to October. Highest rates listed were $4 per day and $25 per week.

5993　　　　　　　LA GRANGE HOUSE, BABYLON, L I.　　　　　　"PUBL. BY HEFFLEY DRUG CO"

LaGrange Inn dates back to pre-Revolutionary War days. General Lafayette visited LaGrange, hence it is named for his home near Paris. Samuel Higbie, early proprietor, operated a stagecoach line between New York City and Patchogue. LaGrange was a stopover on the long journey. In 1915 it was restored and sold to a syndicate of businessmen. It preceded the gilded age and outlived the era of hotels and summer visitors.

Jessie Smith erected the American House in 1780 on the northwest corner of Main Street and Deer Park Avenue. It was a mail coach stop until 1841. The first annual town meeting was held here. Among its famous distinguished visitors were Prince Joseph Bonapart, brother of Napoleon, a former King of Spain, and Daniel Webster, who was on his way to a political gathering in Patchogue.

30

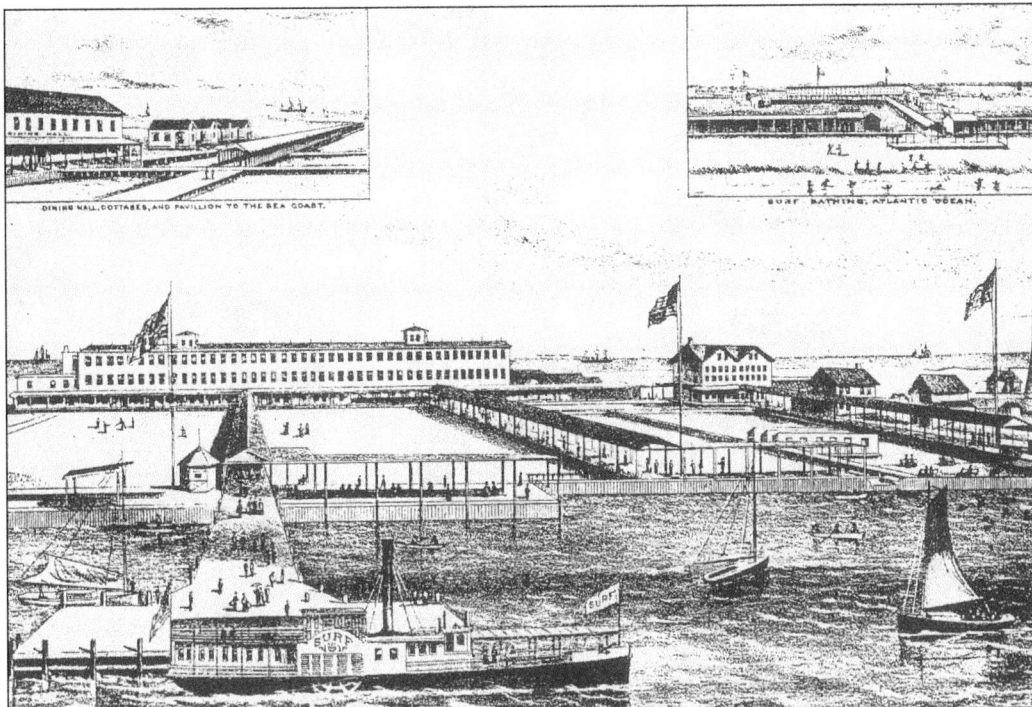

The Surf Hotel was a luxurious establishment conceived by David S.S. Sammis. Completed in 1856 it was situated on Fire Island, east of the lighthouse. Sammis mapped the journey of his clientele from New York City to his lavish hotel. Train, trolley, and ferry would assure him of patrons. The three-story edifice had walks extending to outlying cottages, all illuminated with gaslight. His yacht, *Bonita*, served as a ferry for many years.

David S.S. Sammis, proprietor of the Surf Hotel, first established the East Broadway House in New York City. It succeeded as headquarters for politicians. Sammis became interested in resorts and especially in Fire Island. His palatial Surf Hotel on Fire Island accommodated 100 guests. He installed a trolley line connecting the Babylon depot with the steamboat landing for the convenience of his patrons.

S.C. Smith built the Watson House in 1870. Located on the east side of Fire Island Avenue, it was one of the largest hostels in town. It measured a 133-foot frontage, a 47-foot depth, and a 20-foot-square cupola. The dining room seated 300. The spacious sleeping quarters had ceilings 20 feet high. The Watson was named after a famous comedian. This luxurious hotel was later converted into apartment houses.

The Sherman House stood near the southeast corner of Main Street and Fire Island Avenue. It was situated on the former site of Willets Paper Mill. Sherman Tweedy, the proprietor, was an avid horseman; he rented horses and carriages to his patrons. The hotel accommodated 40 guests in spacious rooms. Patrons enjoyed the advantage of access to the waterfront while living in the village. The Sherman later became Casey's Hotel.

Blue Stocking Inn was located on the southeast corner of Main Street and Little East Neck Road. It had been the former residence of Stanley Foster, president of the Bowery Savings Bank. Foster was an early landowner who donated generously to the Methodist church. He gave the land and then assisted with the building of the church and the interior furnishings.

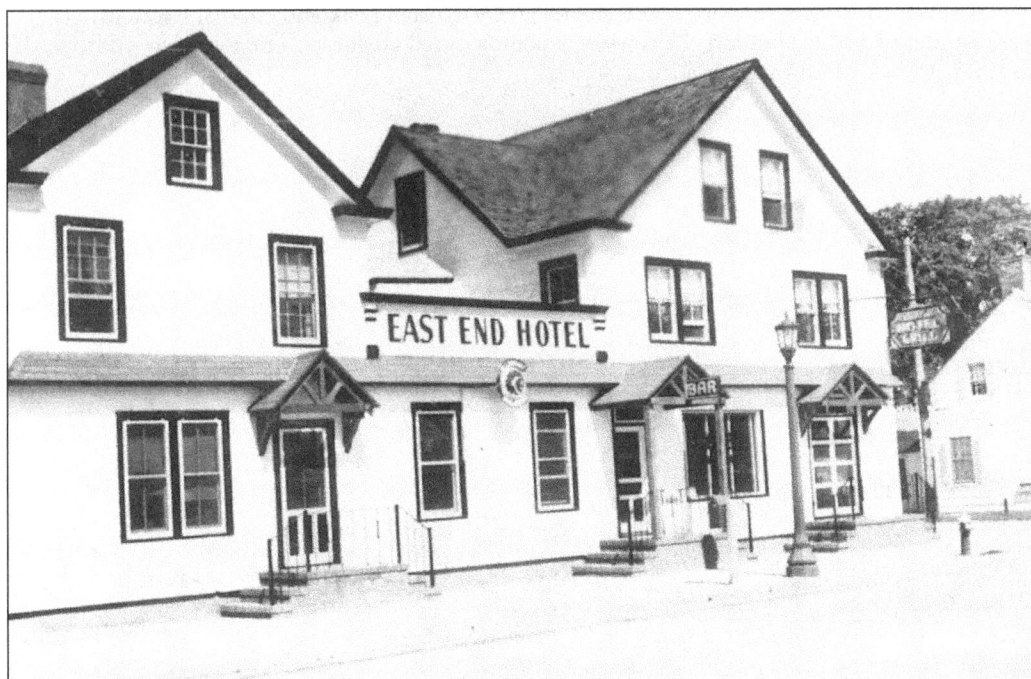

The East End Hotel was established on east Main Street during Babylon's resort days. It outlived many of its contemporaries, and eventually a restaurant was added. Following the decentralization of nearby psychiatric centers, East End Hotel became a welfare haven. In 1982 it was destroyed by fire. A clam and oyster bar now replaces the site where the East End Hotel long stood.

Mr. Hathaway built Hathaway and Newport Inns in 1910. Situated on the mainland at the mouth of Amityville Creek, they served the vacationers who came to summer by the sea. Newport was the larger hotel with four stories and Victorian peak and cupola. For many years it was a landmark for local sailors. Hathaway accommodated 60 guests. The rates ranged from $15 to $20 per week. Both inns perished in a fire.

South Shore Inn was located on Sumpawams Creek. Situated on the corner of Shore Road and Robbins Avenue, it survived the decline of many hostels. This is a 1936 photo.

34

The original railroad station in Babylon included Fire Island. That was the destination of early passengers. Coastal village dwellers recognized the need for a railroad. Some 54 miles of roadbed were laid along the south shore of Long Island, terminating in Babylon in 1867. This created a link with New York and increased the seaside population. It gave rise to hostels on the shore and in the village. The white, wooden historic edifice was razed in 1888.

Steel rails to the east reached Babylon in 1867. On October 11, of that year the first train arrived in town. The round-trip fare was an astounding 85¢. The railroad brought summer visitors to the shore. Horse-drawn carriages met the trains before the days of the trolley. The railroad transformed Babylon into a seaside resort.

The Station, at Babylon, L. I.

The second railroad station was completed in 1888. It was a hub of activity for the seven decades of its existence. No one could predict the eventual pace of commuterism Babylon would encounter. The number of seaside resort travelers eventually decreased, as automobiles became prevalent. Commuter traffic increased and Babylon became a haven for commuters from various villages around Suffolk County.

A trolley operating between Amityville and Babylon Dock transformed the village into a seaside resort. Passengers had to be distributed so that the trolley would stay on the tracks. It clanged along Trolley Line Road through Lindenhurst, Copaigue, and West Babylon and then turned toward the Babylon docks. On one occasion the trolley jumped the tracks at the intersection of Main Street and Deer Park Avenue and struck the drinking fountain, terminating its career.

The R. R. Station and Trolley, Trestle, Amityville, L. I.

A cross-island trolley began operation on August 25, 1909. It ran from the foot of Ocean Avenue in Amityville to Halesite on the north shore. Alfred E. Smith, an annual summer resident and later governor of New York, was the guest speaker for the momentous occasion. Another trolley operated between Babylon and Amityville. Both went out of business when a "passing fancy" known as a motor car or automobile made the trolley obsolete.

Post Office, Amityville, L. I.

The Triangle Building in Amityville was a landmark. Built by Erastus Ketchem in 1892, it was originally crowned by a Victorian cupola. It became a center of activity with the post office and bank on the first floor and the courts on the third floor. It was called "the Establishment." Note the trolley on the left. This was a common mode of transportation between the north shore, as well as Babylon Dock.

37

Rapid Transit to Oak Island, Babylon, L. I.

This was rapid transit of 1871. David Sammis, owner and builder of the Surf Hotel on Fire Island, initiated the Babylon Trolley Line. Sammis completed his hotel and then devised a way to transport passengers to his luxurious establishment. He had tracks laid along Fire Island Avenue to the docks where his steamer awaited passengers to the palatial Surf Hotel.

BABYLON TROLLEY   Published by Winfield B. Gorton, Babylon, N. Y.

The Babylon trolley is leaving the village for Steamboat Dock. The trolley was originally pulled by horses along Fire Island Avenue. Later it became motorized and continued servicing customers until the close of the First World War.

Three

YESTERYEAR

AROUND TOWN

The drinking fountain was built at the intersection of Main Street and Deer Park Avenue. Situated at the village center, it afforded refreshment to man and horse alike. The Women's Exchange donated the fountain in 1897. It was demolished when a trolley coming from a nearby hamlet overturned on it. Heffley Brothers Drugstore is on the northeast corner, and the spire of the Presbyterian Church rises in the background.

The National Bank of Babylon was incorporated on May 8, 1893. Situated on west Main Street, it provided for large-scale operations and initiated business possibilities. Local businessmen organized the bank, and it quickly took its place among widely recognized financial institutions. Transactions were effectively executed to the satisfaction of its patrons. The National was Babylon's first bank.

This corner drugstore stands on the original site of the Conklin House. It was built by G.S. Taylor in 1872 on the northeast corner of Main Street and Deer Park Avenue. It was constructed of Northport hard rock, with a mansard roof. G.S. Taylor opened the drugstore here, and in 1910 Charles C. Heffley took over the business. He operated it for many years and sold his own complete line of postcards.

Main Street, Babylon, L. I. (Copyrighted.)

Babylon was among the first villages on Long Island to adapt electricity. On November 24, 1886, electrical energy illuminated eight stores and three strategically placed streetlights in the village. The first electrical system was generated by Sumpawams Creek hydropower but soon thereafter was moved to larger quarters. Looking east on Main Street the arc streetlight was a welcome innovation at the intersection of Deer Park Avenue and Main Street.

Main Street, looking West, Babylon, L. I.

The concept of an incandescent light hanging over the intersection created a fascination that drew neighboring townsfolk to see the strange, new, modern curiosity. Looking west, Belle Meade Sweets are advertised at Winegar Pharmacy, on the northwest corner of Montauk Highway and Deer Park Avenue. Note the horse-drawn ice wagon on the left.

Elbert Carll was elected first supervisor. Geographic separation was feasible. The rapid growth of the south shore led to differing interests and tensions between north and south. The crucial issue was the construction of an extension of New York Avenue from Main Street in Amityville to Huntington Harbor on the north shore. The cost of this controversial project would be applied to all properties in the town of Huntington.

TOWN HALL AND BABYLON NATIONAL BANK
BABYLON, LONG ISLAND, N.Y.

This is Babylon Town Hall of 1918. Babylon became a town on March 13, 1872. Town board meetings were held in rented quarters for nearly a half century. The estate of David Sammis presented a plot of land on the northwest corner of Main Street and Cottage Place for a town hall. The cornerstone was laid on March 13, 1918, and it functioned at that site for over seven decades.

The present town hall was constructed on Sunrise Highway in Lindenhurst. It was necessary to relocate to larger quarters by 1990. This spacious edifice was built closer to the center of the town of Babylon.

N. Y. State Dept. of Public Works, Babylon, Long Island, N.-Y.   L.I.L. 33

17412

The Public Works Building graces the northeast corner of Main Street and Little East Neck Road. Built in 1940 it was headquarters for the New York State Department of Public Works, District 10. This district comprised Suffolk and Nassau Counties and the five boroughs of New York City. In recent years Greenman-Pederson Contractors has established a business at this site.

43

HEADQUARTERS OF VILLAGE BOARD, POLICE, AND FIRE DEPARTMENT, BABYLON, L. I., N. Y.

The municipal building was constructed on west Main Street. Incorporation of the village took place on December 19, 1893. First proposed in the *South Side Signal* in October 1870, the controversial idea initially created divisions among the citizens! Strife and dissension lingered through the first two attempts, which ended in cancellation. In February 1894 Dr. William W. Hewlett was elected first president, a term that has since been changed to mayor.

The fireproof Municipal Building stands on property donated by J. Stanley Foster. Built in 1925 it is situated on the northwest corner of Main Street and Carll Avenue. The Municipal Building houses the Village Administration, the Health Department and it is headquarters for Police and Fire Departments. The Fire Department was formed on December 1, 1877. The American House stables had burned the previous year. This prompted the initiation of adequate fire protection.

44

Elmer W. Howell entered the village scene in 1891. His hardware business grew rapidly. He operated a builders office, hardware store, and lumber yard for many years. In 1976 the Babylon Historical and Preservation Society awarded Howell the first circa board for the preservation of a building on Deer Park Avenue. The representatives are Jeanne Keeshan, Rosalin Rohl, and Gayle Labenow. This ongoing program recognizes buildings over a century old.

Benjamin P. Field established his business on the southwest corner of Willow and Main Streets in 1853. He was a tinsmith, merchant, historian, plumber, writer, and an inventor with several patents. He remained in business for over a half century while pursuing literary, horticultural, and writing hobbies. In 1889 he sealed a metal box and marked it "Open 1989." His great-great-grandson, Benjamin P. Field V, became heir to the treasure.

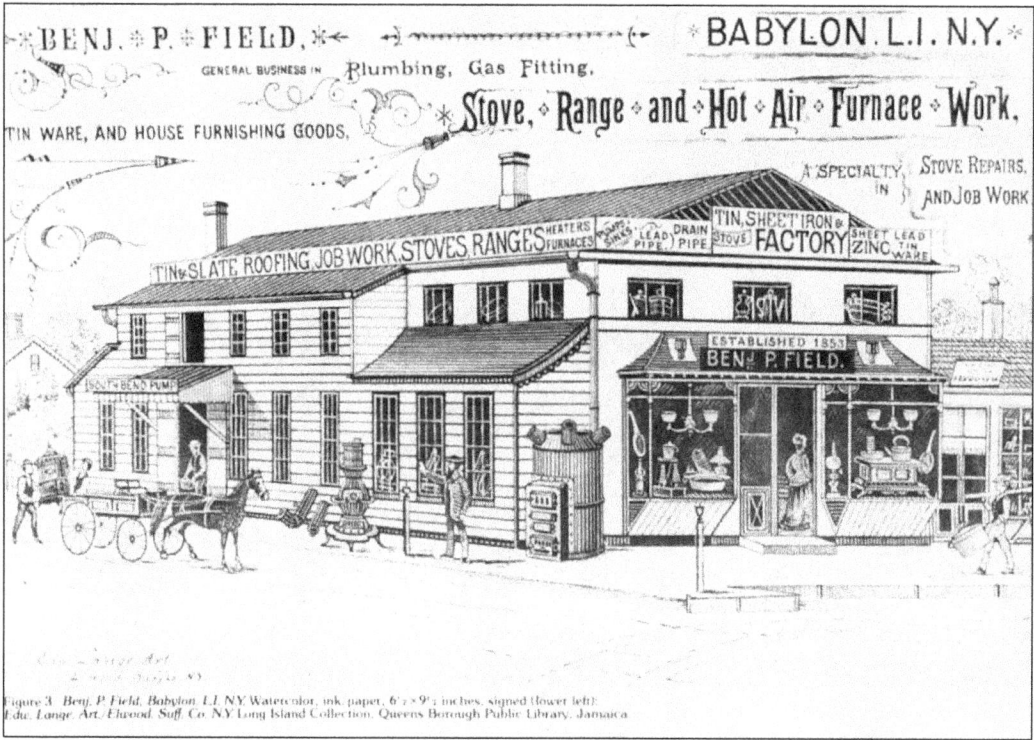

Figure 3. *Benj. P. Field, Babylon, L.I. N.Y.* Watercolor, ink, paper, 6' x 9'; inches, signed (lower left). *Edw. Lange, Art. Elwood, Suff. Co. N.Y.* Long Island Collection, Queens Borough Public Library, Jamaica.

Field's store became a magnet for diverse and sundry products. Field was a master mechanic who was sought after for his unusual abilities. His sense of history led him to preserve a time capsule for his descendants. He published *Reminiscences of Babylon* in 1911, which chronicles early townsfolk who populated the village during a colorful period of its history.

Babylon Bike Shop now occupies the site where Field's store once stood. Field's descendant inherited the century-old treasure. He contacted the National Geographic, which arranged for scanning. At NASA's Space Center the historic box was further analyzed by remote sensing, and in the Boston Laboratory, image analysis was done by computer. It was then decided safe to open the treasure that contained memorabilia and treasures of a century ago.

Main St. and Fire Island Ave., showing Sherman House, Babylon, L. I.

This was the crossroads of Babylon. The Dondon Brothers opened a general store, complete with barber pole, beside the Sherman Hotel. The American Hotel, in the right foreground, includes a public telephone. Note the cupola atop the Sherman House. This gave access to a view of the waterfront from the village.

The Argyle Hose Company early in the century consisted of, from left to right, (kneeling) Forrest Pearsall, William Lerriere, Earnest Everett, Edward Northan, Robert Voss, and Clarence Johnson; (standing) William Bachuda, John Kraft, James White, Selar Baldwin, William Wood, George Davis, Fred Carpenter, Chief William H. Mott, Noah Sprague, Clarence Smalling, William Bonin, Howard Curtis, Albert Davis, Nelson Pearsall, Charles Taylor, John Larned, and John Buschagger.

Education had its beginnings in a one-room cabin schoolhouse on east Main Street in 1802. The lyceum was built on the south side of George Street in 1853 and served as a school for over three decades. The lyceum was also used for public lectures, discussions, concerts, meetings, and other entertainment. A whip factory, roller-skating, and amusements were housed in the basement.

This school building of 1894 served for decades. An escalating population necessitated a new high school. Constructed on the north side of Grove Place, additions to additions were added. The school was growing in leaps and bounds when a fire swept through the buildings in 1957, causing extensive damage. The Joel Cook monument stood in the school yard. Cook was a Revolutionary War veteran.

The present Babylon High School was dedicated on November 10, 1957. All three sections have recently undergone renovations and technological advances. The school, with a student population of 823, provides a variety of courses with access to other resources. It prepares students to confront the challenges of the 21st century.

The elementary school was built on Park and Ralph Avenues in 1954. It was necessary to add an addition a few years later. A new elementary school was built in 1965. Originally the elementary and high schools were housed in the same building.

When talkies became the fad this Capitol Theater was built on west Main Street. It was 1922, and movies were becoming a popular mode of amusement. The theater featured a full stage with live entertainment, as well as movies. Babylon's original theater on Deer Park Avenue could not accommodate the rising number of fascinated patrons. The Capitol functioned for three decades until it was destroyed by fire in mid-century.

Clearview Theaters of Babylon was constructed on the same site as the Capitol. In keeping with theatrical architecture of the day, the Babylon Theater today features three theaters in one. They are housed in a larger, higher, and more elaborate building on west Main Street.

A new horseless carriage chugged into Babylon in 1910. Its sputtering roar attracted the attention of citizens who were curious to see the innovative contraption that could attain the great speed of ten miles an hour. Older folks frowned upon it as a noisy fad. Young lads envisioned themselves someday in such a fascinating style of travel. It provided the interested onlookers with a first glimpse of the automobile.

Dusty lanes and unpaved roads were not conducive to the new motorized mode of transportation. Looking west in 1914, automobiles are on the left, and horses with their buggies are on the right. These would travel side by side for many years. The car is parked at the Sherman Hotel on the southeast corner of Fire Island Avenue and Main Street.

51

BABYLON, L. I. The Road to the Bay.

Strolling along the Crescent afforded opportunity to enjoy the beauties of nature. This charming, although unpaved road was designed to curve gracefully toward Great South Bay. This land, south of Main Street, originally belonged to Captain Underhill, who was a prominent sea captain. He cultivated a huge farm here. Later it was lined with hostels and houses of the affluent and played host to many pleasure seekers each year.

The Girl Scouts march in a "Welcome Home" parade. This practice continued for several years after World War I. The Scouts proudly display the uniform of the era. Early in scouting history young adults were a vital part of the organization. Scouting has always been active in Babylon.

Southside Hospital was initially opened on the northeast corner of Cooper and George Streets in 1913. The first community hospital in Suffolk County, it was converted from the home of James B. Cooper. The building had served as a boardinghouse and a day school before it became a hospital. A more feasible location for Southside Hospital was found in Bay Shore, and the hospital was moved in 1923. This site is now the Babylon Post Office.

The Southside Hospital nurses' residence was on Cooper Street. In this picturesque setting it served the hospital for over a decade and continues to grace Cooper Street. The mansard roof afforded a view of the Great South Bay and the village of Babylon. This was used by Southside Hospital from 1913 until 1923, when the institution relocated to Bayshore.

Ferries are anchored at Steamboat Dock. Boyne's Hotel was situated at the foot of Fire Island Avenue. This site became a bustling point of convergence where land and water met. Trolleys arrived with passengers for the ferries. Carriages and later cars populated the scene. Boyne's Hotel catered to those waiting for the ferry or the trolley.

John Anthony's On the Water now occupies the bustling site of Boyne's Hotel on Steamboat Dock. John Anthony's caters to weddings, anniversaries, and other memorable events. The spacious building overlooks Great South Bay. Its glassy, scenic architecture creates a sensation of sailing on a luxury liner. It was constructed in the 1980s.

Four

ISLANDS IN THE BAY

Oak Beach afforded a dip in Great South Bay or the Atlantic Ocean. Bathers of 1920 were skeptical of what attire to wear in salt water. They consulted a doctor, who advised dark-colored, woolen fabric. He said the entire body should be covered because dark fabric retains body heat and prevents rapid evaporation. It is less likely to leach away natural body salts, he reasoned.

The elite occupied Towanco Inn on Muncie Island. Dr. Muncie managed the three-story building as a sanitarium. Open from June to October it featured plumbing, hot water, an elevator, gas illumination, and open fireplaces. A freshwater supply was pumped in. The price for guests ranged from $9 per night to $25 per week. The Muncie brothers were not only twins but also both medical doctors.

Muncie Island was dotted with stucco bungalows. These housed the elite and combined the freshwater supply, gaslight, and other amenities Muncie Isle had to offer with the quiet seclusion and privacy that city dwellers were seeking. This exclusive island was situated west of Oak Island. A view of the ocean was always accessible.

The Muncie Island Steamboat ferried passengers to and from the mainland. Muncie Island had its own steamboat. It made the 3-1/2-mile trip across Great South Bay twice a day at 10 a.m. and again at 6 p.m. This schedule coincided with the arrival of the trains in Babylon. This was a scene at Steamboat Dock on August 12, 1916.

Surf bathing at Muncie Island Beach was enjoyed by patrons of this exclusive resort. The Island became part of history in the late 1920s when the cottages were floated west to Amityville and the sand was used in the construction of the Ocean Parkway, which became a pleasant drive between Babylon on the east and Jones Beach on the west. The arrow indicates Fire Island.

Landing at Oak Island Beach, N. Y.

The rustic promenade affords a welcome for arrivals on Oak Island. In the 1890s Oak Island was the site of a Methodist camp formed by the Oak Beach Association. It was abandoned when the island became a cottage real estate venture. The first permanent dwelling on Oak Island was that of Henry Livingston in 1879. He called his summer home Little Rest. He was editor of the *South Side Signal*.

The Plank Walks, Oak Beach, N. Y.

The plank walks of Oak Island were a convenience in 1911. Oak Island was originally used for cattle grazing. The sea grass and salt hay were an attractive feature for farmers. As a summer spa it served millions of pleasure seekers over the next several decades. Devoid of commercialism, life was simple without any frills. Homes were connected by these quaint plank walks.

58

Oak Beach Inn was situated amid the sand dunes facing the ocean. Resort hostelries and inns around Great South Bay prospered so well from June to September that prospective occupants were required to make reservations very early to assure desired accommodations. Many families spent leisure time in the sand dunes, as the children found the dunes to be quite a novelty.

Ocean View House faced the Atlantic Ocean on Oak Beach. It was a favorite spa of the affluent and wealthy at the end of the 18th century. Summering on the ocean was the epitome of luxury. Prosperity was on the rise, employment was increasing, and leisure time was a new adventurous commodity few had ever experienced before.

Oak Island Hotel, Oak Beach, N. Y.

Oak Island Hotel ranks among the grand seashore hostelries of the 18th century. This postcard, dated July 9, 1913, was sent from Grace B. on Oak Island to Ella M. in Babylon Village, inviting her to come for another visit. Oak Island is situated northwest of the Fire Island inlet.

Van Nostrand's Pavilion on Oak Beach provided a leisurely stroll on the boardwalk. This was a favorite sport of the ladies with their parasols. Rowboats, anchored nearby, provided opportunity for fishing, sailing, or cruising Great South Bay. The cottages and Oak Island Inn are in the background.

General Store and Post Office, Oak Beach, N. Y.

The General Store and Post Office were on the dunes. This became a social gathering place when the ferry brought the mail from the mainland. Many of the postcards in this collection are postmarked Oak Island. Food was preserved in heavy barrels buried in the cool sands under the house. The ice cream shop was an intriguing innovation on the beach. Legend has it that saltwater taffy was first made on Fire Island by Mrs. Parkinson.

Briggs Store, Oak Beach, N. Y.

Briggs was a general store. Staples such as rice, bread, cereal, milk, butter, and cookies were always available. Produce cost 5¢ more than on the mainland. This paid for its transport across the bay. Shopping for meat and vegetables was done in Babylon once a week. An order was left with the butcher, who put the order aboard the steamer for pick up at the beach.

Oak Beach Chapel was built in 1900 to serve the many summer visitors to the resort area. It was a nonsectarian house of worship. Nearly every denomination worshipped here at some time.

Cottages dotted the sand dunes along the Oak Island shoreline. These afforded privacy, rest, and quiet, except for the peaceful and gentle sounds of the ocean rolling in. They were often the summer homes of the industrialists and tycoons who could afford to summer on the sea. Note the marshlands and salt hay in the foreground.

WAUKEWAN CANOE CLUB, AMITYVILLE, LONG ISLAND.

The Waukewan Club of Amityville was a small group of athletes who had their clubhouse in the famous Establishment or Triangle building. They were especially interested in canoeing and had very large canoes. They paddled all over the bay at speeds of 6 to 8 knots and often canoed east to Babylon for lunch.

The Yacht Club at Oak Beach initiated the season with water sports and a parade in 1916. Oak Island was a grazing land in very early times. In 1879 Henry Livingston built a cottage on the island thus initiating its lurid career as a summer resort. Streets were named for shipwrecks. Many seasonal dwellers built summer cottages beside the sea, while others were weekend visitors.

Regatta Day found many sailboats, rowboats, and speedboats in competition on Great South Bay. It was always a festive occasion throughout the town, and crowds gathered at the shorefront to cheer on the competitors. A sailboat was sometimes considered "Queen of the Bay."

Boating on the Amityville Creek was the equivalent of taking a drive in the country. The creek provided a safe and calm harbor for a leisurely ride. It is one of many creeks, necks, and inlets along Great South Bay.

House, Oak Island, Off Babylon, L. I.

Made in Germany for Hedley Drug Co., Publishers, Babylon, L. I., N. Y.

This house with a lookout tower belonged to Ralph Howell Sr. It was located on the eastern end of the island and afforded a view of the ocean. Approaching ships could easily be sighted from this vantage point.

U. S. Life Saving Station, Oak Island Beach, N. Y.

The Life Saving Station on Oak Island faced the ocean. Patrolmen were on the alert for ships in distress. Patrolmen had their own codes of communication through flashing signals. Previously it had been a practice for coastal fishermen and farmers to watch isolated stretches of shoreline and report ships in distress. It was called "Shoreline Alert Brigade."

65

A lifeline is prepared by the lifesaving crew on Oak Island. These lines are shot to the distressed ship. The danger of shipwrecks was greatly diminished when the lifesaving stations were posted every 4 miles along the shorefront. A trained crew kept vigil beside the ocean throughout the winter and in the storms of summertime.

U. S. COAST GUARD STATION NO. 84, OAK BEACH, N. Y.

Coast Guard stations on Oak Beach were busy all winter. A crew would assemble at their respective stations and establish themselves for the winter. Specific routine practices were followed. They practiced drills, intra-costal signals, apparatus operation, and the revival of victims.

Coast guardsmen use torches to flash emergency signals to a ship in the midst of a raging storm. The torches warn the crew members that they are close to land and assure them that help is near. There is danger of capsizing and also of running aground in the sand.

A lifeboat is brought ashore by a happy crew. These are members of the Life Saving Service, whose duty was beach patrol. Lifesaving huts housed lifeboats, apparatus, and crew, and had adequate space for survivors of shipwrecks. The Coast Guard was not called such until 1915.

The *Bodo* was a fruit steamer from South America containing 20,000 bunches of bananas. It went aground at Hemlock Beach on March 20, 1906. When word reached the mainland that crates of green bananas were washing ashore, everyone headed for the beach. The banana boat was eventually floated in by tug. Wagon loads of bananas were salvaged, banana recipes were created, and one of the churches featured a Banana Pie Festival.

The *Roda* was a 350-foot steamer from Spain carrying a heavy cargo of copper ore. On February 13, 1908, it hopped a sandbar and was stranded near Tobay Beach. Its crew refused to leave the ship, hopeful that tugboats could dislodge it; however, a severe storm forced the crew and captain ashore. The *Roda* is among the many shattered hulks buried in the ebbing sands of Great South Bay.

The *Ripple*, coming in, Oak Beach, L. I.

The *Ripple* is approaching Oak Island dock. The Babylon-Oak Island ferry was the idea of Captain Charles E. Arnold in 1886. He was keeper of the Life Saving Station and was desirous of populating his sandy domain. He began service using a large, black catboat that made two trips a day.

In 1909 Captain Norman Smith entered the ferry service. In 1913 he launched the double-decker *Henry Ludlow*. It was considered the epitome of luxury on Great South Bay.

Waders are enjoying Babylon Beach in 1920. Swimming is considered a fad and not an especially healthy one.

TILE SWIMMING POOL, BABYLON BEACH, BABYLON, L. I. N. Y.

The village pool was constructed at the foot of Fire Island Avenue in 1923. Located on a filled-in meadow site, it was a saltwater pool owned by Babylon Beach Inc. In 1987 the pool was rebuilt, tiled, and filled with fresh water. It measures 80 by 200 with depths from 2 feet to 9 feet for diving. It was purchased by the village in 1949 and named the Gilbert C. Gilhanse Village Pool in honor of an esteemed former mayor.

Parking was a challenge even in 1930. This view from the pier of Babylon Beach in September of that year indicates the rising need for parking spaces. The Model T was in its heyday. People were beginning to use cars for pleasure as well as for work. The era of the parking lot was in its prime and clearly showing evidence of its necessity.

The *Columbia* was a double-decker ferry. It plied the waters of Great South Bay with Captain Frank Wicks at its helm. The fare in 1906 was 75¢ round-trip between the mainland and Hemlock Beach Pavilion. This dock was owned by Westley Van Nostrand, who embellished his oceanfront property by installing bathhouses. His establishment served oyster stew, clam chowder, soft drinks, and coffee to the many passengers patronizing the *Columbia*.

The Channel, Oak Island, N. Y.

The channel, a natural stream of water in the bay, presents a picturesque scene. Fire Island may be compared to a vast stage. Many plays have been enacted upon its soft, white sands: Piratical escapades of earlier times, romantic moments, harsh sea tragedies, and always the alluring awareness that brought generations of visitors back to its shores each year.

The Babylon Rebellion of 1892 was sparked by the arrival of European ships carrying diseased immigrants. The government designated Fire Island a receiving station. Citizens along the bay were intensely dissatisfied and threatened to destroy the steamers. They stationed themselves on the island armed with shotguns, eel spears, pitchforks, and other weapons. A militia was sent to guard the waterfront. Here a regimental supply train arrives in Babylon with provisions for the militiamen on active duty.

72

Five

Babylon Taking its Place in History

Marconi's Wireless Telegraph Station was situated near Fire Island and Virginia Avenues. It remained in operation for two years very early in the 20th century. The small shack in the foreground housed his equipment. This is the first known ship-to-shore wireless relay station in the world. Marconi was awarded the Nobel Prize for his work developing wireless telegraphy. His success as a scientist led to a succession of honors.

Gugliemo Marconi was an Italian inventor. Born in Italy he was interested in radio waves and traveled extensively in pursuit of furthering his experiments. In 1899 he came to New York. A year later he made his major geophysical development in Babylon. He had contacted ships at sea and they had responded. The wireless was born. Marconi received an honorary degree from Columbia University in 1922.

The Marconi shack housed one of the world's first wirelesses. Edwin Armstrong bought the shack and planned on exhibiting it at the 1930 World's Fair in Chicago, a project that never materialized. He presented it to the Radio Corporation of America (RCA) in Rocky Point, Long Island. Standing beside the famous shack in the bottom photograph, Marconi and Armstrong discuss its destiny. Armstrong is the inventor of frequency modulation, the FM radio.

The famous shack stands today in the school yard of the Joseph Edgar Intermediate School on Rocky Point Road in Rocky Point, Long Island. This is also Route 25A. The little white building, which remains intact, measures 12 by 14. Surrounded by a chain-link fence, three windows face the east and the installers Marconi used remain under the ceiling. Josiah J. Pulling visited the historic site in 1982.

THIS IS THE SITE OF THE BIRTH OF THE AMERICAN WIRELESS. A PIONEER STATION HERE IN 1901 FIRST TALKED WITH SHIPS AT SEA.
GUGLIELMO MARCONI

This historical marker was placed on the southeast corner of Fire Island and Virginia Avenues. It is situated near the site where the little shack stood. The marker is a reminder and commemoration of the historic communication that is part of Babylon's history.

10:—L. I. R. R. Station, Babylon, L. I., N. Y.

Steam engines puffed into Babylon for nearly six decades. Railroads had become the traditional mode of travel; however, modernization was on the rise. An historic electrification of the railroad would make Babylon one of the busiest passenger lines in the country. This is a status the village still maintains.

*Y*OU are cordially invited to ride on The First Electric Train carrying passengers between New York and Babylon, on

WEDNESDAY, MAY 20TH, 1925

Special train will leave Pennsylvania Station at 2.15 P.M. and stop at stations named on back hereof at times stated. You can board train at Pennsylvania Station, or at your home station. This card will admit you.

Returning, special train will leave Babylon at 5.20 P.M., and will stop at stations named.

THE LONG ISLAND RAILROAD CO.

GEORGE LEBOUTILLIER

VICE-PRESIDENT

No.

The first electric train left Penn Station, New York City, and traveled along the south shore of Long Island. It was hailed with much applause and jubilation at each station, for it created a faster and more efficient link with New York City. The trip to Babylon took 1 hour and 20 minutes. It was May 21, 1925.

76

A great crowd gathered in the railroad area to witness the arrival of the first electric train. St. Joseph Church is in the right background. The floats of those days were also advertisements. These are arriving from the parade on Main Street and rolling west on Railroad Avenue. Homasote building board for homes, as well as for poultry houses, was demonstrated on these truck houses.

Main Street was crowded during the electrification ceremony. The railroad was electrified to Babylon, which meant speedier service to and from the metropolis. This called for celebration. Parades, bands, and fireworks were in order. Such festivities created a quite common, modern phenomena, a traffic jam.

A police booth was installed at the crossroads. The intersection was decorated with flags and buntings in celebration of the first electric train. Note the "Boatman's Association" and "Public Bath" signs posted on the southeast corner. The steeple of the Presbyterian Church rises in the background.

Babylon's electric train drew an avalanche of daily commuters from surrounding villages. Cars were parked at the depot while their owners traveled to the city. The third rail, which contained the power that propelled the locomotive, is visible on the left of the steel rails. This scene of October 1930 is facing west.

78

Babylon had become "Commuterland" by mid-century, when traffic congestion had reached its peak. The electric line was serving thousands of commuters daily, requiring additional trains. A modern station on ground level replaced the depot of 1888. In the early 1960s, tracks were laid along a culvert that carried the trains above the street. Numerous commuters no longer interrupted traffic.

A VIEW FROM THE SEAPLANE BASE, BABYLON, LONG ISLAND, N. Y.

Lawrence Sperry was an aviation pioneer. He built the world's first guided missile and then demonstrated it for U.S. Navy Personnel on September 11, 1916. It was called the Sperry Aerial Torpedo. A historic marker on the southwest corner of Unqua Street and Richmond Avenue in Amityville attests to this historic event. In 1920 Sperry built the first seaplane in Farmingdale and tested it in Great South Bay at Amityville.

Queen of the Holy Rosary Academy was opened by the Dominican Sisters as an elementary school for orphans and neighborhood children. It later became a boarding school for young ladies. The site was destined for yet another ministry. The Sisters settled on an Amityville farm in 1876. The motherhouse was eventually established here. The Dominican Community had its origins in Germany. The first band of four sisters arrived in New York on August 26, 1853.

St. Albert Hall was originally built as a Sister Formation College in 1956. This plan, instituted in many congregations, met with an unpredicted turn of events. A sharp decline in religious vocations necessitated a strategy change. The building now houses the administrative offices of the congregation and a large, well-equipped infirmary. The Dominican Sisters of Amityville established Molloy College in Rockville Centre in 1955.

Dominican Village now stands on the site of the former academy. A vast complex of golden buildings house the elderly. This huge, magnificent residence was dedicated in May 1993. It employs the most modern technology in caring for golden-agers. Care of the sick orphans, the elderly, and children have always been among the special work of the Dominican Sisters.

The house of James Thorne stood on Main Street. A butcher by trade, his shop stood beside his residence. Acclaimed as an excellent judge of livestock, he was noted for keeping the best quality meats. Each autumn he would show the largest, healthiest hogs in the country and was sought out for this talent. His was one of the first businesses to install electricity. His son George continued the business until about 1910.

St. Joseph Roman Catholic Parish dates back to the early 1850s, when services were held in homes. In 1877 Rev. Joseph Coughlin built the original church, this small wooden edifice on Grove Place facing the present rectory. The little church was attractively decorated and provided a prayerful atmosphere. The seaside community, however, experienced a rapidly growing Catholic population. A larger house of worship was proposed.

St. Joseph's Church was constructed on the southeast corner of Grove Place and Carll Avenue. Bishop Charles E. McDonnell celebrated the first Mass on July 28, 1912. One year under construction, it is modeled after San Stafano of Italy in Byzantine architecture. The marble mosaic altar was shipped from Italy as a gift of Mrs. Arnold Constable, who financed much of the project. The generous benefactor was a member of the Arnold Constable retail chain.

The magnificent edifice gracing the village was the only St. Joseph's Catholic Church in the Diocese of Brooklyn in 1912. The dome is 80 feet high and is a replica of that in the Sistine Chapel. The church has a total length of 125 feet and contains over 1.5 million bricks. Facing the church on the left is the drop-off entrance for the horse and buggy.

St. Joseph School was opened in 1927 with an enrollment of 240 students in six grades. The Sisters of Mercy, whose motherhouse is in Dallas, Pennsylvania, staffed the school during its 64 years. The first graduation took place in June 1930. The school was then complete with eight grades. The enrollment continued to rise over the years reaching a peak of 1,200 by the early 1960s. In 1972 a new wing was added, containing classrooms and a library.

83

St. Joseph Convent was erected in 1927 to house the Sisters of Mercy. The architecture of the building matched that of the rectory. The original convent was situated on what would become a vast parking lot. The 1950s and 1960s witnessed the greatest growth when enrolled parishioners numbered 5,500. With the rising population, additional faculty was needed. More than 152 Sisters have at sometime taught at St. Joseph's. Many lay teachers joined the faculty.

The Sisters of Mercy moved into the new convent in July 1971. The chapel is on the right, the parlor and porch on the left, and the stairwell tower leads to the roof. This vantage point affords a panoramic view of Babylon Village. The spacious edifice accommodates 24. The original convent was demolished, and the site became an expansive parking lot. St. Joseph's rectory is in the left background.

St. Joseph Church and School celebrated together in 1977. A centennial Mass of Thanksgiving was celebrated by Bishop John R. McGann, with native son Msgr. Thomas Leitch as homilist. It marked a century since St. Joseph's Parish was established. In that same year the school was observing a half century of service to the Catholic population of Babylon. Rev. John Gorman was pastor during this milestone era.

St. Joseph's 50th first grade entered the school in September 1977. The schoolchildren are, from left to right, as follows: (first row) Scott Riley, Maurice Moodie, Emmanuel Mora, Michael McLaughlin, Thomas Fergueson, Victor Osborne, Lawrence Knapp, and Ralph Tomeo; (second row) Karen Forsythe, Anne De Matteo, Kelly Markham, Nicole Frigano, Monique Parrish, Nancy Kresa, Jean Lurie, Denise Scott, Linda Johnson, and Kristen Galewski; (third row) Malina Karagiannis, Thomas Vasiliou, Scott Slayton, Derek Panza, James Dour, Paul Federico, Anthony Zuyderhoff, Alex Montalvo, Matthew Crowley, and Michelle Ferell; (fourth row) Sr. Mary Ildephonse, Robert Stallone, Anthony Spadolini, Stephen Buetow, Lorenzo Bencini, Nicholas Capezza, Paul Kelly, Terence O'Brien, Martin Maloney, and Sr. Anne Frances.

Charles Bishop owned and operated a music store for many years. He carried a complete line of postcards that were made exclusively for his business. Bishop was also a musician who added life and animation to the village. He joined a group called Company A, 16th Regiment, NY State Militia, commanded by James B. Cooper. The group made credible appearances in drills and parades.

4821   BISHOP,S MUSIC STORE. BABYLON N.Y.

From Herman Ewert.

West Main Street, Babylon, L. I., N. Y.

Diagonal Parking was common in 1930. This scene is looking west along Main Street. A restaurant stands on the southwest corner, and the second Babylon Theater is beyond that on the left. The radio shop, the First National Bank, and the columns of town hall are visible on the right. The arrow in the foreground leads one south along Fire Island Avenue.

86

Parades, complete with decorations, have always been a favored activity in Babylon. Here, Warta's Band is turning onto west Main Street from Deer Park Avenue. This parade commemorated Independence Day in 1917 and was followed by a flag-raising ceremony. Note the trolley tracks that provided transportation between the railroad station and the Babylon dock.

Independence Day parades were a custom for many years. In 1918 this horse-drawn fire wagon, a replica of earlier times, joined in the festivities. Note the fire extinguisher on the wagon.

H.C. Grand Economy Store was known as a Five & Ten. It was a popular store in the 1930s. Emil Steyer's Upholstering and Decorator business shared part of the building. He also advertised cabinet making. A sign on the Maindiner stated "Ladies invited."

Winters of long ago were colder with greater snowfall than we have today. A risky feat on the icy waterfront exemplified just how frigid the weather could become. The winter of 1933 was unusually cold, and Great South Bay was frozen solid from shore to shore. Here a family has parked their car and are standing on the bay to demonstrate the strength of the ice.

Six

ON THE SHORES OF GREAT SOUTH BAY

Babylon was the Tulip Capitol of Long Island. Bulk's Nursery was established in 1921 by Jack Bulk and situated on west Montauk Highway. In 1929 he constructed a windmill. It was a reproduction of a mill in his hometown on the Rhine in Holland. The windmill added an atmosphere of enchantment to the area for many years. It was the original site of tulip festivals. Bulk's offices were housed in the windmill, which was demolished in 1983.

Tulip time called for a parade. This was held in conjunction with the Tulip Festival every spring. The Babylon High School Band and twirlers proudly performed. Delighted bystanders, some from neighboring towns, enjoy the festivities. C.J. Van Bourgondien of Hillegom, Holland, founded Van Bourgondien Importers of Bulbs and Perennials. His sons, Karel and Peter, brought the business to Babylon in 1919.

A little Dutch cottage is hauled in the annual Tulip Time Parade in 1950. A replica of a typical dwelling in Holland, the float is complete with tulips planted in the flower boxes. It is traveling south on Deer Park Avenue and will terminate in Argyle Park.

The springtime Tulip Festival created a joyful spirit in the town. It drew many visitors who came to appreciate and enjoy the beauty of these flowers. Flower girls, dressed in native Dutch costume, distributed tulips to the spectators. The Tulip Festival was created by two local importers who made their homes in Babylon, the Van Bourgondien Importers of Bulbs and Perennials and the Bulk Garden Center.

Tulips are admired on the west side of the municipal building. Flowers were both imported and exported and were used in the annual Tulip Festival. They were distributed throughout the village, giving it an attractive, charming atmosphere.

Van Bourgondien Importers' impressive offices and warehouse are located on Route 109. Products are shipped to and received from many foreign countries. They are often sold under the name Hans Brinker. The present patriarch of the business is Fred Van Bourgondien, son of Karel, who joined the business on the American side of the ocean in 1940 when he completed duty in the Dutch Army.

Cornelius Van Bourgondien was the first of the family to explore Babylon. He came in 1904 then later returned and built this lovely Dutch house on Albin Avenue in 1935. The building currently serves as St. Pius X House of Prayer. It is administered by the Sisters of St. Joseph. The house with the present Van Bourgondien Park and playground is situated on the original site of the growing fields.

The G.M. Weeks family settled on east Main Street before the turn of the century. They were among the first to establish a garage and car salesmanship. Situated along the south side of Main Street, they specialized in Buick cars. The Buick was developed by a Scottish inventor in Detroit. David Buick built the first Buick car in 1903. It was a two-cylinder car, marketed as the Model F. Note the pole in the foreground for tying horses.

William Hogan pauses before going on duty. As a police officer his daily task was to guide schoolchildren across Deer Park Avenue. In the 1930s when a few cars constituted heavy traffic, this was a practice throughout the county. The site is at the Tooker and Harnell Garage on Railroad Avenue. Note the convertible Ford, running board, narrow tires, and single gas pump. The driver is fascinated with the motorcycle.

The Alhambra Theater is on the left, looking south along Deer Park Avenue in 1915. Situated on the second floor of the building, it was an entertainment center for villagers. It also served as an auditorium for graduations.

The steamer is loaded at the Babylon Dock. It prepares to transport passengers and cargo across Great South Bay during Old Home Week in 1910. This took place annually following a parade and celebrations on the mainland. Summer dwellers on Oak Island would come across the bay for such occasions.

94

A parade commenting Old Home Week is wending its way south on Deer Park Avenue in 1910. Townsfolk turned out to celebrate. The wagon on the right advertises Drakes Bakery. Parades in the early days attracted spectators from nearby towns and villages. Decorating the buildings with buntings and patriotic banners was a common practice because it added to the festivities.

In the early 20th century Babylon had an affinity for parades, tournaments, and homecomings. On August 20, 1910, the horses pull the hook and ladder at the northwest corner of Main Street and Deer Park Avenue during the parade commemorating Old Home Week. The buildings in the background comprise the old Post Office Block.

PUBLIC LIBRARY, BABYLON, LONG ISLAND, N.Y.

Babylon Public Library had its beginnings in 1887 when several women formed a Book Circle. They paid dues, bought books, and circulated them among charter members. In 1911 a library building was constructed on land donated by Elbert Livingston. Situated near the northeast corner of Main Street and Carll Avenue, the spacious building now houses the Babylon Historical and Preservation Society. Note the Baptist Church on the left.

The new public library was constructed on South Carll Avenue in 1968. Designed to accommodate the population, it contains 9,100 square feet of usable space with shelving for 39,000 books. The building contains a large, spacious reading area, children's section, and circulation department. Many services are available in the library.

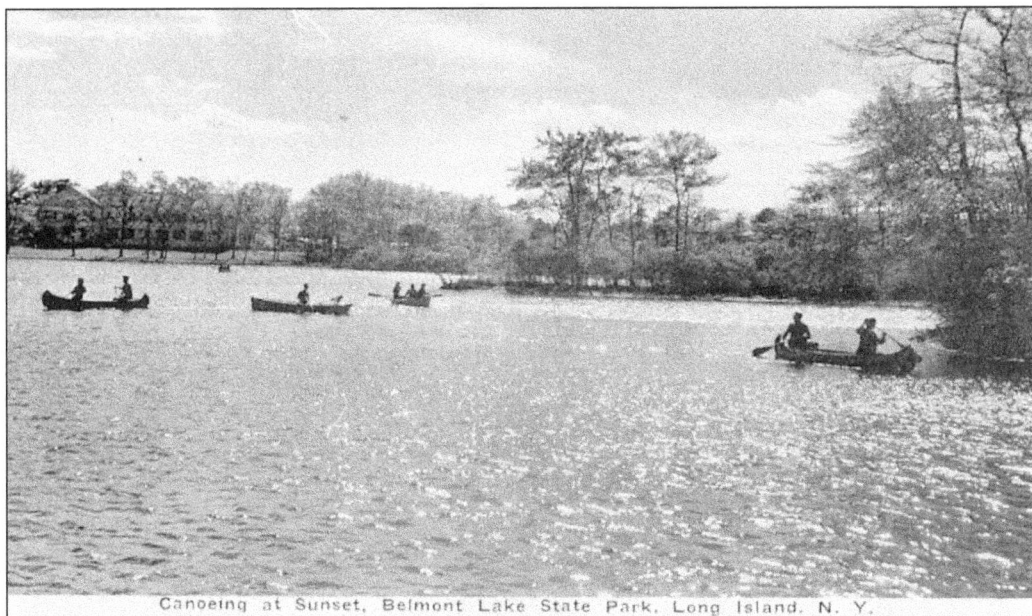

Canoeing at Sunset, Belmont Lake State Park, Long Island, N. Y.

Canoeing was a popular recreation on Belmont Lake. August Belmont, a German-born financier, bought 1,100 acres of North Babylon property, including a 40-acre lake, in 1864. He was an ardent horseman and developed a stud farm with extensive stables. His horses were English imported. His contemporaries dubbed Belmont a financial wizard. His millionaire status is attributed to an apprenticeship in the House of Rothchild, the leading Jewish Banking House in Europe.

Lake Scene, Belmont State Park, Babylon, L. I., N. Y.

Belmont Lake became a mecca for pleasure seekers. Boating was prevalent on the lake. Housing was provided for 50 stable boys with a building large enough for equestrian winter workouts. One half of Belmont's acreage was to feed the horses. In 1925 New York State bought 459 acres for a State Park. This postcard was sent from Andrew to his folks in the city, while he worked on Belmont Lake in September 1930.

97

Greetings from Belmont Park Aviation Field, Babylon, L.I.

U. S. AVIATION TRAINING FIELD.   SERIES NO. 12   222670

Belmont Aviation Field was created from Belmont Park during World War I. The estate became a training area for fliers used by the Army Corps with an encampment of 1,200 soldiers. The army used 280 acres including the famous mile-long track. It was formerly opened on June 13, 1918. Belmont's villa, overlooking his trout preserve, later became headquarters for Long Island's State Park Commission and the State Police.

DEER PARK AVENUE—LOOKING NORTH
BABYLON, L. I., N. Y.

Deer Park Avenue was paved by 1930. Note the lampposts lining the avenue. This same site witnessed horse racing, trotting, foot racing, greased pig chasing, sack racing, and many sports of a very early era. On this lane the once famous trotting mare Lady Suffolk showed that she was the fastest trotter of the day c. 1850.

98

MAIN STREET, BABYLON, L. I.

The Red Cross was always promoted throughout the village. In the early days of the organization, banners were placed along Main Street. This banner was hung across west Main Street in 1922. The Sherman House is in the left foreground. The famous Conklin House on Deer Park Avenue was the original headquarters for the Red Cross in Babylon.

The Red Cross contingent is turning west. They are marching south from Deer Park Avenue onto Main Street. This is a parade after World War I. Women turned out to join the war efforts and to do their part in service to humanity.

The *Babylon Beacon* office was established on Deer Park Avenue. Edward and Jane Wolfe founded the newspaper in 1966. The first local newspaper was the *South Side Signal*, founded by Henry Livingston on July 9, 1869. In 1911 James B. Cooper II established the *Babylon Leader*. Out of circulation since 1965, this newspaper has recently been revised. During the last three decades, the *Babylon Beacon* has been keeping townsfolk abreast of local happenings.

Weight Watchers International is housed in this spacious building on the southeast corner of James Street. Built by Silas Udall in 1870 on land purchased from Simeon Cooper, its Victorian architecture provides a widow's watch. The building was sold to the Honorable Walter Scudder and then passed into other hands until 1970 when it became Weight Watchers Headquarters of Suffolk County.

Erastus H. Munson donated the first ambulance to the village of Babylon. He was owner of the Grinell Lithographing Co. of New York City. This was, at one time, the largest greeting card company in the world. Munson moved to Babylon in 1921 and became active in the civic and political life of the community. Oliver C. Grinell founded the Grinell Lithographing Co. in Bayshore in 1908. It was later called Munson Card Co.

The American Legion has always been active in Babylon. The post commanders in 1945 were, from left to right, as follows: (front row) L. Squires, A. Mac Quarrie, T. Newton, C. Easton, T. Dooley, J. Tennis, W. Redfern, J. Ettinger, and H. Reilly; (middle row) J. Spillane, F. Abbott, W. Brown, P. Ott, E. Strohsahl, C. Rogers, and B. Slosberg; (back row, standing) T. Morris, A. Downs, C. Birs, C. Hogan, G. Durkee, D. Haggerty, E. Ryan, C. Baum, R. Corbert, M. Sumner, and P. Ricketts.

Babylon has always had an active police department. The Babylon Village Police Department of 1948 consisted of, from left to right, (front row) Hank Smalling, Chief Russell Grover, Jim Nolan, and Tom Murray; (back row) Sam Atkins, Philip Corso, Bill Walsh, Herb Bruhl, and Jim Pearsall.

South Country Road, Babylon, L. I.

The C.M. Bergen House was originally situated on Montauk Highway. It was moved around the corner, south, to Thompson Avenue. It is situated on a site once occupied by the Robert Moses residence. The Argyle Commons complex now occupies that site.

RESIDENCE OF MRS. WM. ARNOLD, BABYLON

The Arnold estate was established in West Islip in 1872. Richard Arnold chose West Islip as his summer home. He was enthralled with the dry goods business. He and his brother-in-law, James Constable, joined in partnership. This resulted in the Arnold Constable Department Store chain. The Arnold mansion, built in 1906 by Annie Constable, is located just north east of the exit ramp from Robert Moses Causeway.

Oak Neck Road, Babylon, L. I.

Oak Neck Road connects Montauk Highway with Great South Bay. Located in West Islip, the entire area was once part of Babylon. Just east of Robert Moses Causeway, the spacious Oak Neck is one of the many necks along the South Shore. Prior to 1873 the writer, W.L. Andrews Esq., built an estate on Oak Neck and modeled it after the home of Henry Wadsworth Longfellow. Today the area is known as Pace Landing.

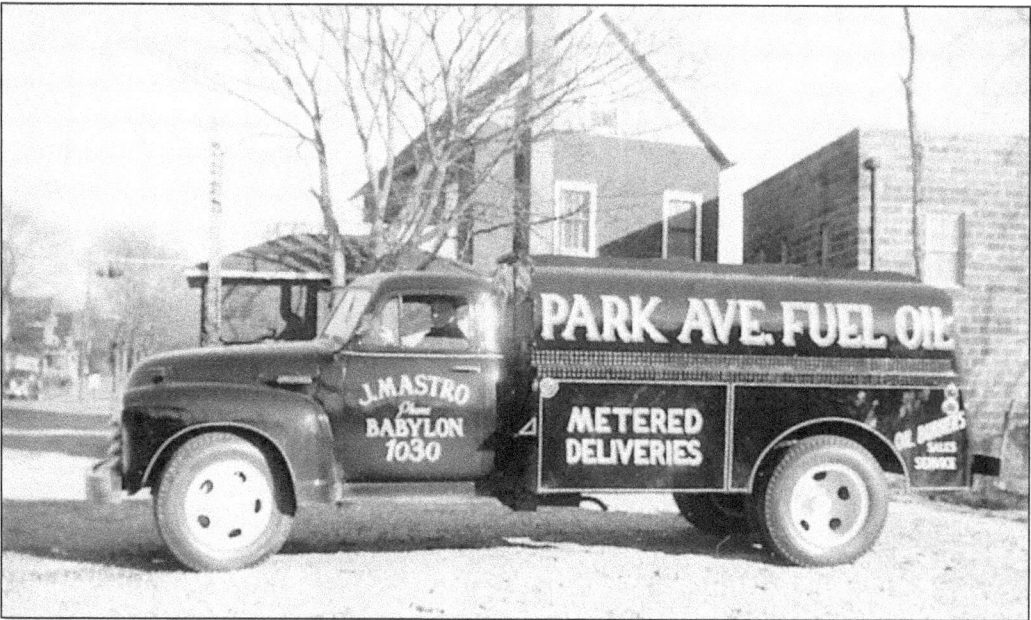

Joseph Mastro delivered ice from the ice plant he bought on Park Avenue in 1939. In the era of refrigeration he added fuel, coal, and oil. A huge 275-gallon oil tank was sunk along Route 109, and the fuel business prospered. His daughter Lena, wife of Albert Sweeney, took over the business. It is evolving into a third generation enterprise. Presently, Joseph and Albert Sweeney Jr. are in the business, which has relocated to Evergreen Street.

Grandma's Kitchen was established in the original Park Avenue Fuel building. The Mastro family resided here, and this was Antoinette Maestro's kitchen. Her granddaughters, Nancy and Lee Anne Sweeney, opened the little ice cream shop in the 1980s. Few can pass by the triple-decker ice cream cone without pausing for refreshments. Homemade products are a specialty of the little shop.

Speakers gather for the United Nations Rally held on September 20, 1947. The United Nations Booth was set up in front of Babylon Theater. A Legion bugle corps. parade preceded the rally. The speakers were District Attorney Lindsay R. Henry, Charles Pfeifle, who represented the Babylon Rotary Club, and Gilbert Hanse, who represented the mayor.

Rev. Monsignor Thomas A. Leitch was in the first class to complete eight years in St. Joseph's School. He graduated from Shippensburg State College and Purdue University. He served in the Army Air Corps as a pilot during World War II. Leitch was ordained in 1955 from St. Mary's Seminary, Baltimore. An outspoken critic of nuclear power, he was a priest, pastor, principal, and vicar general in the Diocese of Harrisburg, Pennsylvania. He died in 1983.

William Dzus was a native of the Ukraine. He became a shrewd businessman and inventor. In the 1930s he developed an ingenious fastener that is secure, vibration proof, and affords quick access with security and dependability. Used initially on aircraft, it quickly became the choice in all fields of industry. Dzus held numerous patents for his inventions. His has become a third-generation business.

Remember Captain Kangaroo? He is Robert Keeshan, who lived in Babylon. Keeshan first acted in a school performance and then became an NBC page at Radio City Music Hall in New York. On October 3, 1955, Captain Kangaroo premiered on the CBS-TV network. He is the winner of five Emmys. The show survived for three decades and became the longest running children's program on TV. His approach is appreciated by generations of adults and children alike.

Former Mayor Gilbert C. Hanse is a graduate of Babylon High School. He is a charter member of the Lions Club and the Masonic Lodge #793. He served as fire chief and as mayor of the village twice, for a total of 33 years. He served as supervisor of the Town of Babylon from 1965 to 1970. Projects he initiated include conversion of the pool to fresh water, elevation of the railroad, founder of Little League, and the historical society.

Former Congressman James Grover was educated in Babylon, Hofstra, and Columbia Law School. He had a four-year tenure as an Air Force Captain in China during World War II. He spent six years in the New York State Assembly before serving as a congressman for 12 years. The Congressional Record applauded him as a "Patriot of total integrity." Currently the statesman has returned to his local law practice.

Bret Saberhagen of Major League Baseball joined the Kansas City Royals. In his nine years with them he received the World Series championship, Most Valuable Player, Golden Glove Award, and two All-Star awards. He was traded to the New York Mets where he attained all-star status. Four years later he was traded to the Colorado Rockies. Presently he is a member of the Boston Red Sox. Saberhagen lives in Babylon with his wife, Lynn.

BRET SABERHAGEN

Hapi and Crissy Auer operate the Glen Dinette on East Main Street. They serve breakfast and lunch in an atmosphere that transports one back to rural Main Street. The little dinette with its counter and stools also features many photos of old-time Babylon. Amid the memorabilia preserved is a menu of Zanetti's Candy Kitchen in the 1930s, when a cup of coffee was 5¢ and a sandwich 15¢.

108

Seven

Into the
New Millennium

This aerial view of Babylon was taken prior to 1957. The railroad parking lot in the upper center is filled. Cottage Row winds back to Grove Place. Note the original town hall, the bank, and the Presbyterian Church. The high school with its 1927 addition faces Grove Place, and St. Joseph's Complex has no additions yet. Babylon Cemetery is in the extreme upper right. The crossroads are Deer Park Avenue and Main Street.

Senator Owen H. Johnson is a resident of West Babylon. A graduate of Hofstra University, he began his distinguished career in 1972 when he was elected to the state senate. He is presently president pro tempore, the second highest-ranking position in the state senate. He has authored numerous laws in the fields of social services and environment. Johnson is the second resident of the town of Babylon to serve in the senate. The first was Richard Higbie (1896–1898).

Richard H. Schaffer was elected supervisor of the Town of Babylon in November 1992. He is a graduate of the State University at Albany and Brooklyn Law School. He was also president of the Tulip Acres Civic Association. He serves the most densely populated township in Suffolk County, with over 205,000 residents, and is the youngest supervisor in its 126-year history. Schaffer successfully stabilized town property taxes. He resides in Lindenhurst Village.

E. Donald Conroy is a native son. A graduate of St. Joseph's School and Babylon High School, he served four years in the Navy and then attended Champlain College and Hofstra University. A 45-year member of the fire department, he served two years as fire chief. In 1975 he was appointed to the Village Planning Board and served ten years as a trustee. He was elected mayor in 1987 and continues to serve in that capacity.

Robert Moses was born in New Haven, Connecticut, in 1888. He was a wizard of the park system. He attended Yale, Oxford, and Columbia before becoming State Park commissioner. His monuments are legion. Southern State, Jones Beach, Ocean Parkway, Captree, Belmont, Long Island Expressway, Varrazzano Bridge, and Throggs Neck Bridge are just a few of his masterpieces.

111

The Bank of Babylon was established in 1913. This impressive white building on the west side of Deer Park Avenue was built in 1922. The bank flourished here for over six decades. In 1986 it became the Bank of Long Island and in 1989 the Bank of New York.

The Babylon Beautification Society has retained a quaint charm in the village. Flowers are suspended from Victorian lampposts that illuminate the main thoroughfares. The centennial clock is a gift to the village. The Beautification Society arranged to purchase the Smith & Derby clock from England. It was installed on the northwest corner of Deer Park Avenue and Grove Place on December 28, 1992. Note the lamppost in front of Loman's Store.

Anthony and Mary Spadolini brought Wellwood Memorials to Lindenhurst. In 1947 they bought property on the northeast corner of Route 109 and Wellwood Avenue in Lindenhurst. Mary operated the monument business in the area, while Anthony kept the monument business on Staten Island. Wellwood Memorials is now entering a third generation, and the same fine service continues to prevail. Mary Spadolini, the family matriarch, continues to assist in the business.

John Eppig was a hotel manager in the area. His wife was skilled in preparing duck dinners. In the advent of prohibition and desirous of going into business for himself, John became interested in flowers. The era of hotels in the area was ebbing into history, so John established the Eppig Florist. It prospered and expanded to become a prominent florist along Montauk Highway in West Islip. His son Louis later took over the business.

Good Samaritan Hospital Medical Center opened as a 175-bed hospital in 1959. Situated on a 60-acre site overlooking Great South Bay in West Islip, the facility has expanded through five major additions in the past four decades. It serves the towns of Islip and Babylon in numerous and diverse ways, while providing quality health care to all its patients. Surrounding communities benefit from the wide scope of its services.

St. John the Baptist Diocesan High School was established in West Islip. Situated on Montauk Highway, the school opened on September 8, 1966, with 672 freshmen. The plant covers 24 acres and is fully accredited by the Board of Regents of New York State. Enrollment has soared into the thousands. The fully equipped modern building includes a huge auditorium, a library of over 20,000 volumes, and a 1,200-seat gymnasium.

Michael Rice established the Ancient Order of Hibernians (AOH) in Babylon. A native of County Mayo, Ireland, he founded St. Patrick's Division Two in 1946 with 24 members. Meetings were held in various locations as membership grew. In 1970 the organization purchased a hall on Locust Street, where the promotion of Irish culture could more readily be achieved.

The Irish Cultural Center on Locust Avenue was renovated and enlarged in the 1980s. Hibernian members remodeled, expanded, and beautified the building to accommodate a rapidly growing membership. A decade later the Golden Jubilee of the AOH was celebrated in the refurbished hall. This has always been a very active Irish center for Babylon as well as surrounding towns and villages.

The Saffron Kilt Pipe Band was founded by Matthew Close of County Antrim in 1962. The bagpipes were played initially in the 1965 Memorial Day Parade. Two years later they joined the St. Patrick's Day Parade in New York City. In 1980 they performed for President Carter. The band consists of 50 members with a full color guard. It is considered one of the best bands in the country. The trophies and awards the band has received are legion.

Matthew Close, founder and pipe major, Eleanor Wallace, past president of the Ladies Division, and Robert O'Shea, drum major, pause for a chat. The Ancient Order of Hibernians were originally those men, during penal times in Ireland, who guarded the priest while he was offering the Mass for the people of a locality. This often took place in the fields or woodlands because Catholic churches were outlawed in the country.

A color guard leads the Saffron Kilt Pipe Band west along Montauk Highway. This is the annual St. Patrick's Day Parade in East Islip. The Saffron Kilts took part in the All Ireland Piping Championships. They played in Dublin, Kerry, and Kilkenny Castle and were invited to Glasgow, Scotland, where they competed with over 200 bands. They were featured at the Rose of Tralee Festival. In 1990 the Saffron Kilts performed at Radio City Music Hall in New York.

Matthew Close, pipe major, and Robert O'Shea, drum major, with piper Hank O'Neill stand at attention. The Saffron Kilt uniform, with green jacket, is modeled after the official kilt worn by members of the pipe band in the Army of the Irish Republic. The Saffron Kilt Pipe band has earned respect and admiration for dedication, musical skills, charitable contributions, and the promotion of Irish culture.

The Ladies of Division Two are marching on Fifth Avenue in the St. Patrick's Day Parade. The ladies' division of the Ancient Order of Hibernians was first organized in 1958. They are involved in every aspect of Hiberninism. They run fund-raisers and have been active in the Saffron Kilts, Irish stepdancing, and Hibernian choir. Many charitable organizations have been the beneficiaries of the ladies' auxiliary.

The Ancient Order of Hibernians took part in the Bicentennial Pageant. Jack McKeon directs as they perform patriotic songs and orations. Sr. Anne Frances of St. Joseph's School faculty paints a verbal picture of the Irish immigrant sailing into New York Harbor where the "torch of liberty stood aloft as a beacon and welcome beside the golden door of freedom." The group impersonated newcomers to our shores in dress as well as in song.

118

The Hibernian Players were organized in 1977. John Burke brought the first play back from Ireland. Entitled *The New Gossoon*, it provided distinctive entertainment and extraordinary talent. *The Swan Song* was produced the following year. The cast included, from left to right, (front row) Pat Rattigan, Eileen O'Hara, and Anne Keane; (standing) Mike Flanighan, Jim Sullivan, Stephen Feeick, and Jack McKeon. It takes time, energy, and enormous effort, but members of the cast enjoy producing the plays.

Anne Dent, shown here with Michael Flanighan, is recognized for her work behind the scenes. She does all the makeup for the players in all of the plays. Prompting, lighting, carpentry, and photography are all necessary to produce such entertainments. A behind-the-scenes crew, made up of Hibernians, execute these tasks and keep the plays running smoothly.

The Winning Maid was produced with the following members, from left to right, (front row) Betty Close, Anne Keane, and Eileen O'Hara; (back row) Mike Flanighan, Willy Quinn, Stephen Ferrick, Brendan McDonald, and Jack Kean.

Don't Bother To Unpack consisted of, from left to right, (front row) Patricia Rattighan, William Quinn, Patricia Kanary, Eileen O'Hara, and John O'Brien; (back row) Brendan McDonald, John Keating, and Leo Murphy.

Kelly Love and Shannon Love Vandette demonstrate their Irish heritage at the Babylon Craft Fair. An Rince Mor School of Irish Dance was founded in 1974. Among the original students were Mary McKay, Margaret Sayre, Anne Mulligan, and Patti Love Vandette. They went on to teach Irish step dancing at the Cultural Center. Through the efforts of Patti Love Vandette the program has spread to other parts of Long Island.

The gazebo becomes a stage for Katherine Nyland, Christine Chambers, Anne Schellhorn, Keri Chambers, and Marybeth Schellhorn. The An Rince Mor dancers play a major role in community entertainment by performing numerous shows for a variety of audiences. They have competed locally, nationally, and in world championships. This performance was part of the annual Crafts Fair.

121

A local rendition of "Lord of the Dance" is presented for the Merchant's Fair. An Rince Mor School of Dance is represented by Anne Schellhorn, Keri Chambers, Patricia Love Vandette, instructor, Eileen Schellhorn, Caitlin Schellhorne, and Patricia O'Hara. The dance was performed in October 1998. Patricia Love Vandette has been teaching Irish step dancing to generations of students. She keeps the culture alive through dance.

A choreography of the mummers, complete with scarves, is presented in the Cultural Center on the occasion of their tea party and recital. An admiring audience looks on. The champions are represented by, from left to right, Dympna Lynch, Amanda Lynch, Juliette Saman, Shannon Vandette, Patricia O'Hara, Eileen Schellhorne, Anne Schellhorne, Caitlin Schellhorne, Keri Chamber, and Christine Chamber.

In 1996 the Ancient Order of Hibernians celebrated a half-century as St. Patrick's Division Two in Babylon. Festivities were in order with a special Mass of Thanksgiving in St. Joseph Church, followed by a parade and dinner. The clergymen concelebrating the Golden Jubilee Mass were: Deacon John Morrow; Rev. John Gorman, former pastor of St. Joseph's; Rev. Jerry Twoomey; Rev. James Kissane, chaplain; Rev. Virgil Power, former chaplain; Rev. Tomas Maloney; and Rev. Frank Nuss.

The Golden Jubilee celebration brought this spirited trio together. Fr. Virgil Power, formerly of County Waterford, a longtime pastor in the diocese was also chaplain of the Hibernians. Ireland's Golden Voice, Frank Patterson, who takes his audience on tour via video, is a native of Clonmel, County Tipperary. Patrick Keane is a longtime member of the AOH who conducted a weekly Irish radio show for many years. His hometown is in County Clare.

Captree Bridge was opened in 1954 by Robert Moses, State Park commissioner. It spans Great South Bay to Captree State Park, which is the home of the fishing fleet. The marine basin, fishing piers, and waterside picnic grounds are located here. Charter and private fishing boats are anchored at Captree. The park lies at the eastern tip of Jones Beach Island. A second span, on the right, providing two-way traffic, was opened in 1968.

A 1955 view of Captree State Park overlooks the sand dunes and the Atlantic Ocean. Cars reached Captree for the first time in 1954. There was space for 500 vehicles. Prior to the bridges, charter boats and ferries serviced the island. Patrons shown here used the new Captree Bridge.

124

The sparkling waters of Great South Bay have always provided a sheltered, inland waterway for marine life. We think of the bay as a source of recreation. In the early days it was the livelihood of our pioneer ancestors. Today it is harbor for swimming, boating, clamming, fishing, water skiing, and narrated sight-seeing excursions. The parking lot accommodates 1,700 cars.

Ferryboats were common on Great South Bay. Regular passenger service was maintained between Babylon and Fire Island until the causeway to Captree was complete. A Rapid Water Service Shuttle between Babylon and Fire Island served passengers until the inlet was bridged in 1964. This scene was taken shortly before the devastating hurricane of 1938.

125

Fire Island Bridge is also known as Robert Moses Bridge. It spans the famous Fire Island Inlet. Constructed in 1964 the bridge terminates on Robert Moses State Park, which is the western tip of Fire Island. A 202-foot-high water tower with a 1,102-foot well was completed in 1968. It holds 313,000 gallons of water. The Coast Guard Station and Lighthouse are east of the water tower.

Robert Moses Bridge affords access to the most southerly outpost on this continent: Fire Island. This project terminated Moses's dream to build a parkway along the length of Fire Island. There is no road today between the Fire Island Lighthouse at the western end and Smith's Point at the eastern end of the island. Democratic Point is the western tip of Fire Island. The space between the two bridges is called the Jones Beach Barrier Beach Island.

126

Ocean beaches on Fire Island attract thousands throughout the summer. The luxury of swimming in the Atlantic Ocean or just lying on the beach of white quartz sand is facilitated by the easy access of the bridges. The building houses a refreshment stand, dining areas, and bathhouses. A broad, white sandy beach connects land and water.

Long Island is home to millions of sea gulls. They are gregarious birds who catch food while flying, stay near land, and gracefully soar around the fishing boats. Their piercing chatter "klaw-klaw," a familiar seaside sound, is often directed to any human who they suspect in possession of a morsel of food. Each evening they congregate in a large nesting area designated for them at Captree.

127

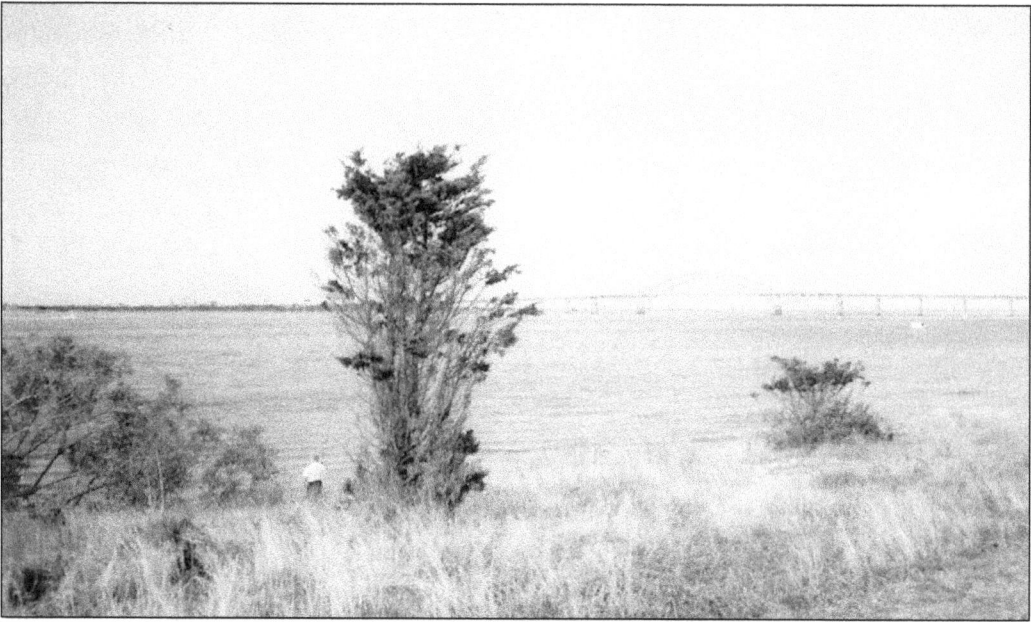

A lone fisherman tries his luck in this glance back toward the mainland. Standing on the shore of Robert Moses State Park on Fire Island, he faces north and looks back at the Robert Moses Bridge he has just crossed and the mainland. It is several miles from the mainland to the park. In order to reach this point, a series of bridges have been crossed.

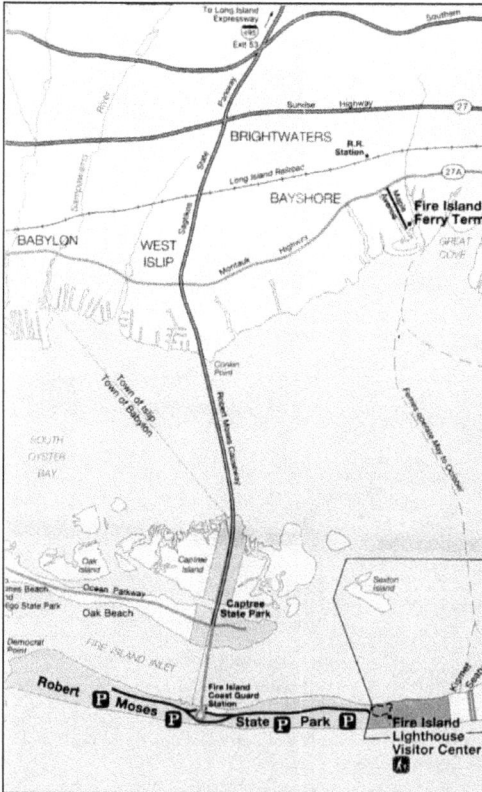

This map details the proximity of the islands, parks, beaches, and bridges to each other.